Second Thoughts

Second Thoughts

On Having and Being
a Second Child

LYNN BERGER

Translated by Anna Asbury

Henry Holt and Company

New York

Henry Holt and Company
Publishers since 1866
120 Broadway
New York, New York 10271
www.henryholt.com

Henry Holt® and 🌸® are registered trademarks of Macmillan Publishing Group, LLC.

Library of Congress Cataloging-in-Publication Data

Names: Berger, Lynn, 1984– author. | Asbury, Anna, translator.
Title: Second thoughts : on having and being a second child / Lynn Berger ;
    Translated by Anna Asbury.
Other titles: Tweede. English
Description: First US edition. | New York : Henry Holt and Company, 2020. |
    Includes bibliographical references.
Identifiers: LCCN 2020039712 (print) | LCCN 2020039713 (ebook) |
    ISBN 9781250787866 (hardcover) | ISBN 9781250787873 (ebook)
Subjects: LCSH: Second-born children. | Subsequent pregnancy. | Brothers
    and sisters. | Families.
Classification: LCC HQ777.22 .B4713 2020 (print) | LCC HQ777.22 (ebook) |
    DDC 306.85—dc23
LC record available at https://lccn.loc.gov/2020039712
LC ebook record available at https://lccn.loc.gov/2020039713

Our books may be purchased in bulk for promotional, educational, or business use. Please contact your local bookseller or the Macmillan Corporate and Premium Sales Department at (800) 221-7945, extension 5442, or by e-mail at MacmillanSpecialMarkets@macmillan.com.
First US Edition 2020

Designed by Meryl Sussman Levavi

Printed in the United States of America

10 9 8 7 6 5 4 3 2 1

For E. and O., of course.

Love set you going like a fat gold watch.
The midwife slapped your footsoles, and your
   bald cry
Took its place among the elements.

—Sylvia Plath, "Morning Song" (1961)

Contents

Preface

Expecting

Ask a person why they want to have a child, and the answer is likely to involve a nebulous tangle of deep longing, curiosity, and something to do with "nature."

Ask why they want another, and the response tends to be rather more straightforward. "You have your first child all for yourself," I was told when big and round and heavily pregnant, "but you have the second one for the first."

We were sitting on the edge of the sandpit then. It was summer, and my daughter was busy with buckets and spades. I cannot remember anymore who it was exactly who told me so. My own mother, perhaps? What I do remember is the effect those words had on me: my head spun with questions great and small, and I began to feel a little queasy.

Eight months previously, we'd been sitting in the bathroom, me on the toilet, my partner and daughter on the cold tiled floor. It was five days to her second birthday. I'd placed the test by the basin, the window facedown for extra suspense. A minute's wait.

When I turned the stick over, it told me what I already knew, what my body had already realized.

My partner smiled, sheepishly, as did I. I think we were both looking for the appropriate response, one that would do justice to the enormity of the revelation—but my daughter was growing impatient. She wanted to go outside, or at least move on to the next thing. To stretch the moment out a little, I took a quick snapshot, hasty and somewhat blurred. In it, my partner is holding the test up in one hand while his other arm lies protectively around our daughter's waist. She's frowning into the camera, one pudgy little arm cast dramatically against her forehead.

The test, of course, meant nothing to her. But projection has always come easily to me, and when I look at that photo now, I can still detect something more ominous in her expression than a toddler's waning interest. Irritation, perhaps, at what we'd done, or anxiety at what was about to happen.

○

What was about to happen was, to us, a couple living in the Netherlands, far from exceptional. Where the average Dutch woman around 1860 had four children, a hundred years later that number was down to three. And after 1970, the number dropped below two.

Since then, for a number of reasons, including female

emancipation, birth control, and the state of the economy, women have continued to postpone motherhood by small increments, and the number of large families has continued to shrink. Nevertheless, one thing has remained constant for the last half century: two is the norm. Of the Dutch people who actually have children, the majority desire and achieve a "standard family" with two children.[1] As in lots of other European countries, as well as in the United States, a two-child family is currently both an ideal and, for many, a reality.[2]

After all, as a friend of mine once irreverently summed up the going consensus, "An only child is a lonely child."

We were on the brink of becoming a standard family. The countdown had begun, the countdown to the norm. (And the norm, I realized, was a privilege. Even if a nuclear family with two parents and two healthy children was the most ordinary thing in the world, it certainly wasn't to be taken for granted—or exalted, for that matter.)

○

My second pregnancy was planned and very much desired. Like many parents, I wanted my daughter to have a brother or sister, a playmate and an ally. I had more selfish motives too. I wanted to experience the adventure anew—the transformation of my body, a freak show with myself in the lead role, along with everything that would follow: holding a newborn baby, the wonder at their unfolding, getting to know that new creature.

Like the first time, the discovery, or confirmation, really, that I was pregnant left me elated and excited. I recognized the nervous tingling you get when you've said yes to something big, whose consequences you can't fully fathom—along with the thrill of possessing knowledge that, to the rest of the world, is still a secret.

In contrast to the first time, however, the excitement pretty soon made way for thoughts and feelings I hadn't anticipated.

While somewhere deep within me my son was starting out on his stunning evolution from tiny clump of cells to prehistoric creature to fetus, I began to wonder what his impending arrival would mean, precisely.

What did it mean, for my partner and me, to have a child *for the second time*? Our first had been nothing less than a miracle, an event without precedent for us, but what did that make our second? A repetition? A perpetuation? A trip down memory lane?

What did it mean for our firstborn, that soon she would no longer be the sole recipient of our time and attention, no longer the only object of our affection?

And what did it mean for my son, to be born into a family that already existed, that had already found its modus operandi, and therefore couldn't or wouldn't revolve around him alone?

My son's movements first became perceptible at winter's end. They began as vague vibrations from deep within, faint like the underground signals emanating from an earthquake hundreds of miles away. Soon they turned into caresses, and those caresses became the unmistakable somersaults of a miniature human being.

Don't worry, those somersaults seemed to say: *I'm moving, I'm alive, I'm on my way.*

I had been looking forward to this quickening, but the sensation wasn't purely reassuring. I noticed that I spent less time observing his stirrings than I had with his sister. The reason, of course, was that selfsame sister: she distracted me, consumed my time as well as my thoughts, and in all her childish innocence utterly exhausted my energy reserves, substantially diminished as they were by pregnancy.

My son hadn't even been born yet, and already I was giving him less attention than I would have liked.

You have your second child for your first. By the time I heard that phrase, in the summer, by the sandpit, I had no trouble identifying the unease it engendered. In fact, wasn't the big question what the firstborn would get out of it, exactly? As for what the expansion of our family would do to our actual family life, again, I had no idea. And the precise effect on the second child was similarly uncertain.

Only long after I'd embarked on my maternity leave, and it had grown so hot outside that staying indoors seemed the only option, did it occur to me that certain assumptions lay at the foundation of my thoughts and feelings about my second pregnancy.

The assumption, for instance, that a child is better off with a brother or sister than without. But also that with the arrival of the second, we were not just *giving* our first child something; we were taking something away as well. And there was the assumption that our second, who would never experience the exclusivity of which we were about to deprive the first, would start out with a one-to-zero disadvantage.

Second place, consolation prize, runner-up.

Those beliefs had to come from somewhere. It seemed to me that it must be possible to find out where they had originated, and to what extent they were justified.

I couldn't understand how I'd failed to consider these assumptions before. But isn't it always the way? You think you know what you're doing, only to be surprised by the discrepancy between concept and execution, between idea and reality. And isn't experience, often, a prerequisite for reflection, so you can only wonder what things mean when you're slap-bang in the middle of it all—when there's no way back?

○

There are entire shelves filled with books on parenthood—from fairy tales, novels, and memoirs to polemics and collections of essays. I have a pretty good lineup in my own bookcase. But while I was expecting our second child, I realized that we have surprisingly few words for this particular new experience. Most reflections on parenthood are about the wonder and inundation occasioned by the birth of a first child—about the transition to parenthood. What happens when another one comes along is hardly ever the focus of contemplation.

It's as if we prefer to talk about the revolution rather than the restoration; innovation and surprise rather than the same old song. The literature on the subject has a great deal to say about the excitement of the first time but falls silent when it comes to the joy of repetition.

And surely all that is fair enough: never is the impact so great, the shock so severe, as when you have a child for the first time. You've stumbled into the world of parenthood from one moment to the next, and once there you can never return.

But if two is the norm, isn't it time to ask, what about the second time? What does it mean to have a second child, and what does it mean to *be* one? Isn't it time to bestow words on the issue of how things continue when you bed down deeper into this new reality, the reality of family life?

○

In looking for answers to my questions about second children, I delved into the work of psychologists, biologists, neuroscientists, and demographers. The empty spaces in my bookcase began to fill up, and continued to do so long after my son had arrived. And the more I read, the more people I spoke to, the more I understood that I also needed to look much closer to home. Literally so—because experience sometimes becomes its own answer.

Second Thoughts is the result of a quest that took place in the scientific literature as well as in my own home. This book came into being because of something to do with nature, curiosity, and, above all, deep longing: the burning desire to better understand the second time, the second child.

Second
Thoughts

"There's going to be a baby"

A brief history of jealousy

During the spring in which I'm pregnant with my son, my father presents my daughter with a picture book. *There's Going to Be a Baby*, it's called, by John Burningham and Helen Oxenbury. The story begins when the main character, a little boy, is told by his mother that she has a baby in her tummy. The pages that follow depict the fantasies spun in his mind, fantasies about what will happen once the second child is there.

In one of these fantasies, the baby is a chef, turning the kitchen into a total mess; in another, the baby appears as a banker, literally throwing money around. When the baby features as a zookeeper, chaos ensues.

"Can't you tell the baby to go away?" the little boy wants to know. "We don't really need him, do we?"

Night after night, I read the book to my daughter. I try to gauge whether her feelings are as mixed as those of the protagonist, but she's not giving much away. Her interest is drawn to the mother's patterned dress, the large ice-cream sundae served to the little boy at a café, and the various names of the animals at the zoo. As far as I can tell, the main message has passed her by; it's just the details that have hit home.

I wonder about the intended readership for this book. Who, exactly, needs preparing—and what for?

○

It might be one of my earliest memories: my little sister, suddenly there. I had just turned three at the time and was convinced, somehow, that my parents were wrong about her name.

Thinking back to her arrival, it's that apprehension that has most remained with me, the certainty that she was really called something else, and that it wasn't in my power to correct the mistake.

In the years that followed, my sister and I mostly argued—constantly, relentlessly, to the point of physical violence, tooth and nail.

"Your characters clashed," is the way my mother puts it now.

"You found me irritating," my sister says.

Or maybe I was just jealous.

○

The first biblical murder—that of Abel, by Cain—is the result of sibling rivalry. Many of Shakespeare's plots revolve around envious brothers and sisters. And in the big book of *Grimms' Fairy Tales*, from which I regularly read to my daughter, jealousy between children of the same family is a recurrent theme.

It's an astonishing paradox: while we believe growing up with a brother or sister to be a good thing for a child, we've also, for centuries, been telling stories about the ways siblings can make each other's lives miserable.

"For a long time I regarded my little sister as an intruder," wrote US author Helen Keller in 1903. "I knew that I had ceased to be my mother's only darling, and the thought filled me with jealousy." In her autobiography, Keller describes the time when, in a fit of rage, she overturned the cradle, little sister and all: "The baby might have been killed had my mother not caught her as she fell."[1]

"A fat, monstrous creature had suddenly acquired the main role," wrote director Ingmar Bergman as he recalled the birth of his younger sister. Little Ingmar failed in his attempt to strangle the baby—his autobiography throws up a vivid image of the time he climbed onto a chair to get at her cradle, but slipped and fell to the floor.[2]

A friend who, like me, is the eldest in her family, tells me about an old video recording in which her younger sister, just learning to walk, proudly clambers up off the kitchen floor and wobbles toward the camera—only to be brutally thumped on the head by my friend's clenched fist.

Can't you tell the baby to go away? We don't really need him, do we?

Prior to my second pregnancy, it seemed to me that the expansion of our family held only advantages for my daughter. I kept thinking of my sister and myself: of how no one has such an intimate understanding of where I come from as she does, how there's no one with whom it's so easy to compare notes on my parents as with her, and how lovely it is to be known, and to know someone, in that way.

I had wanted my daughter to have the same thing: an ally. But now, with spring coming to an end and that ally about to emerge, my thoughts begin to reach further back. Specifically, to our childhood. And it's there that the image becomes much less appealing, because our childhood fighting didn't come to an end until I left home for college, the ravages of a decade and a half of sibling warfare smoldering in my wake.

What made me think a second child was such an unequivocally good idea?

In the evenings, my daughter asleep, I click my way through a pastel-tinted online parenting forum, followed by similarly pastel-tinted parenting websites and mothering blogs. It's easy to get lost here, in this Wonderland, where the tone switches with astonishing ease from reassuring to alarmist and back. "You will feel worse than you did the first time around," I read, for example, in a list of "Ten Things No One Tells You About Having a Second

Baby," and, "the same things that sucked before will suck again." Yet I'm also told not to panic, because "you will be 110 percent more chill about everything."[3]

My son gently kicks me from inside. I stroke the bump as I read on.

Online, I soon notice, second children are often presented as a potential problem: they put even more pressure on their already tired parents, throw family routines into disarray, and above all they provoke a series of reactions, some desirable, some less so, in their elder sibling.

I'm reading all this because I want to know more about my second child. But what there is to read is mainly concerned with my *first* child: with what I can expect of her when the second one arrives. The outlook varies from a profound lack of interest to extreme anxiety, and from bed-wetting to outright jealousy, Keller and Bergman style.

Obediently, I bookmark the many recommendations on how to deal with the imminent threat. Hounded by adverts, I then order various parenting books to be sent from across the ocean.

Siblings Without Rivalry.

The Second Baby Survival Guide.

Peaceful Parent, Happy Siblings: How to Stop the Fighting and Raise Friends for Life.

Such telling titles. It's as if rivalry and fighting are the norm, and deviation possible only with great effort. As if there's a good chance the second baby will stifle our family, as if it's going to be a struggle for survival when he arrives.

My partner, who's more levelheaded than me, and who remembers a predominantly peaceful childhood with not one but two sisters, raises his eyebrows when the books arrive. How much *more*, he wonders, is all that extra literature supposed to teach us? I tell him I find it calming, the same information, formulated slightly differently each time. Apocalyptic, but clearly presented, and full of practical tips.

I like to think, I tell him, that a universal guide to the arrival of a second child exists somewhere, a primordial instruction manual for the months ahead.

There's advice, for instance, on preparing our daughter in good time for what's coming. We can do this by talking about the baby like he's a "real person," and by reading to her from books like *There's Going to Be a Baby*.

We have to make it clear to her, I repeat to my partner, that the arrival of a second child doesn't mean she's loved any less, and above all we have to let her know that nothing is being taken away from her.

We can start by showing her photos of when she herself was a newborn, so she knows that she, too, drank milk out of a breast once; that she, too, used to bathe in a tiny tub, supported by big hands.

My partner nods, benevolently.

Presents are always a good idea, I read somewhere. I wouldn't want to make things too easy on myself, so one sweltering late-spring afternoon I visit a frenzied toy shop on a bustling street. I navigate toward the pink section, in search of a baby doll we can give my daughter on behalf of her little brother, a gift to break the ice when he gets here.

The one I go for is small, with innocent eyes and a soft little hat on its head.

A cheeky little peace offering.

Standing at the counter I suddenly become aware of myself, pregnant and perspiring, attempting to extinguish a conflict that hasn't even presented itself yet.

Later, much later, I'll find the doll, naked and missing its hat, abandoned lifeless at the bottom of a toy basket. I'll remember that it barely interested my daughter in the first place, that she found her little brother far more exciting. It will become clear to me that the gift said a lot about me and my expectations, and very little about my children.

I'll ask myself how justified it was, my fear of jealousy.

But all that has yet to come to pass. Right now, summer is fast approaching. We need to find a new crib, there are hand-me-down onesies to wash, a cradle to assemble. And in between all those activities, I continue to read up on jealousy.

○

Immediately after William Darwin was born, his father began to make notes. It was 1839, and, besides being a brand-new father, Charles Darwin was also a scientist, with an inordinate interest in the expression of emotions.

In the first week Darwin noted that "various reflex actions, namely sneezing, hickuping, yawning, stretching, and of course sucking and screaming" were "well performed" by baby William. On the seventh day he conducted a new experiment: he touched William's foot with a piece of paper. The baby pulled his leg up and curled his tiny toes—"like a much older child when tickled."

After six weeks, Darwin detected a proper laugh from his son for the first time. At four months, it was clear that William could experience rage. His entire head would turn bright red when he was displeased. The baby was six months and eleven days old when his nurse pretended to cry: William promptly pulled a "melancholy face, with the corners of his mouth well depressed"—an unmistakable sign of empathy, in his father's view. And when William was fifteen months old, and his little sister Annie was born, Charles discovered, while weighing his second child in front of his first, that his son could also be jealous: "Jealousy," he noted, "was plainly exhibited." (He omitted to record precisely how it looked, this exhibition of envy.)

Many years later, when Darwin published his notes in the journal *Mind*, he added that William's expression of jealousy at fifteen months came relatively late. "When tried in a sufficient manner," he suggested, infant jealousy could probably be elicited much earlier.[4]

Darwin was right, I learn when studying a weighty academic tome helpfully titled *Handbook of Jealousy*.

Scientists have yet to agree upon what, exactly, jealousy is—emotion or cognition, or rather a state encompassing several emotions at the same time, including rage, fear, and sadness.[5] What *is* known is that jealousy flares up when we're afraid of losing something or someone to another person.

In that sense it's useful, evolutionary psychologists say: jealousy spurs us on to combat the threat of unfaithfulness, or to put a stop to it once it has started.[6] That's handy if you want to keep your lover to yourself, but also for babies and small children who want to hold on to their parents' attention when a sibling arrives. Early this century, psychologists performed a study in which they arranged for babies of just six months to watch while their mothers held lifelike baby dolls: the babies sulked, frowned, and cried. If the mothers held a book instead of a doll, the little participants reacted with considerably less agitation.[7]

None of this is surprising, I suppose. As far back as the third century AD, Augustine described a baby who couldn't yet talk, but who was clearly "livid as it watched another infant at the breast" of its mother. "Who," Augustine added rhetorically, "is ignorant of this?"[8]

What *is* new, *Handbook of Jealousy* tells me, is the bad rap jealousy is subjected to these days. In the Middle Ages, jealousy was associated with the defense of one's honor, and in that sense was positively regarded. It was also long seen as a natural expression of love and devotion. Darwin, for one, classified little William's jealousy as a sign of affection.

This remained the case for a long time. For his contribution to *Handbook of Jealousy,* historian Peter Stearns consulted old US handbooks, letters, and magazines and concluded that until the nineteenth century, jealousy between siblings simply wasn't something parents worried about.

It hadn't occurred to me that fear of jealousy might be a historical phenomenon, something that didn't arise until a certain time, a certain place. The advice I incant to my partner and myself relates to a threat that one hundred and fifty years ago was not even recognized as such.

The turning point, Stearns writes, came at the end of the nineteenth century. That's when jealousy lost its positive connotations, when it no longer fitted into an ideal vision of civilized adults, who were now expected to repress their impulses.

And because self-control could not be instilled early enough, jealousy between young siblings transformed from something at which parents shrugged their shoulders into a serious problem.[9]

Take Sigmund Freud. He didn't waste a great many words on sibling relations, as he was primarily interested in the bond between parents and children. But what little he did say on the topic was devastating enough: in *The*

Interpretation of Dreams, published in 1899, Freud noted that "hostile feelings towards brothers and sisters" must take up a substantial proportion of childhood dreams.[10]

He later observed that a child "put into second place by the birth of a brother or sister . . . does not easily forgive . . . this loss of place": they become "embittered," an emotion that forms "the basis of a permanent estrangement."[11]

Freud's Austrian disciple (and later dissenter) Alfred Adler believed the arrival of a sibling to be a traumatic event for a child. The first was "dethroned" by the second, and siblings would compete for their parents' attention and approval throughout their childhood.[12]

In the early-twentieth-century United States, rivalry had grown to be such an important topic in child-raising books and magazines, Stearns reports, that one could in fact speak of a widespread "sibling rivalry scare." Parents were advised to nip it in the bud as soon as possible if they didn't want their children to harm one another—or, at least as bad, grow up to be unstable adults.[13]

Even the generally mild-mannered Dr. Benjamin Spock, the bestselling child-rearing expert, cautioned, in the mid-twentieth century, that sibling jealousy should be promptly dealt with. Jealousy, he felt, was incompatible with real love, and could even get in the way of "normal" social relations. Clearly, then, there was every reason to eliminate the malignant condition in childhood.

○

So here's the irony: just as jealousy between children from the same family was becoming a phenomenon to be feared, those very families actually began to shrink. In many industrialized countries, the end of the nineteenth century saw the "demographic transition" take hold: child mortality rates declined and, not long afterward, so did the average number of children per family.

Evolutionary biologists have no trouble explaining this transition. If your children have a better chance of surviving and reproducing, you don't need to have as many to ensure that your genes get passed on to the next generation. Moreover, the fewer children you have, the more time and resources you will be able to "invest" in each of them.[14]

It may be, as Stearns speculates, that children had a greater need for parental attention *precisely because* they had fewer brothers and sisters to play with, and that this automatically increased the rivalry between them. (In the Dutch magazine *De Vrouw*, a parenting advice columnist named Nelleke Bakker remarked as early as 1899 that "bickering" was probably most fierce "in families with only two children, because the children are constantly forced to endure one another's company." A "third element," she added, might serve as a lightning rod.[15])

But above all, the growing attention on, and fear of, jealousy between siblings was part of a new understanding of parenting—one that had arisen in the wake of the demographic transition. Now that illness and premature death no longer formed the main source of parental worry, children's psychological development and well-being became paramount. From then on, the reference book *Vijf eeuwen opvoeden in Nederland (Five centuries of raising children in the Netherlands)* informs me, parents wanted "to be able to give care and attention to each child individually." This, too, was one of the reasons for the shrinking family: ample care and attention "are more easily given when there are only a small number" of children.[16]

Parents thus suddenly found themselves responsible for the *inner* lives of their offspring. And for advice on the matter, they went for the first time not only to grandmom or grandad or the neighbors, but also to a relatively new figure in the child-rearing world: the independent expert. A new group of professionals—pediatricians, child psychologists, and developmental psychologists—possessed knowledge that parents lacked, or thought they lacked.

On the ways in which parents were to combat jealousy, these experts were unanimous. Their methods don't differ all that much from the advice I'm offered today by parenting websites, forums, and guidebooks—this collection of incantations that I can now reproduce without effort:

Acknowledge that the first child doesn't have to be outright enthusiastic about the impending upheaval.
Tell grandmoms, grandads, and other visitors soon after the birth that they should pay particular attention to the eldest.

And if the first child still exhibits jealousy when the second child is born, don't punish them for it—extinguish the emotion with all the love and understanding you can muster.[17]

Of course, the fact that in the twentieth century child-rearing experts began to hand out advice doesn't mean that parents have actually taken that advice to heart. Even so, it seems to me that if anything, all this hand-wringing about rivalry and jealousy has left parents feeling more disempowered than self-assured. In fact, the underlying message, that we're *inflicting* something on our children when we reproduce for the second time, is enough to make us feel guilty and slightly at fault.

Fortunately, a later generation of researchers would set out to put into perspective the doom scenarios of Freud, Adler, and others peddling an outsized fear of jealousy. I'd like to figure out precisely how they did this, if only to assuage my own nagging sense of guilt—but it's the end of August, and I've almost reached my due date.

2

Bad is stronger than good

On the birth of the second child and the resilience of the first

My son is born during a heat wave. At home, like his sister just over two and a half years earlier, and on the same sofa. This time I'm lying the other way around, though, as this midwife is left-handed.

The contractions have been going on for hours when she knocks on our window, sometime after midnight, a blond angel with a doctor's bag under her arm. They go on for hours more, those contractions; only when my daughter, who is still asleep, is picked up bright and early by my sister-in-law does dilation really get going. (My sister-in-law gives me a thumbs-up as they walk out the door; I groan in response.)

The sun is already up when he enters the world at last. Blue, screaming, slippery.

"You've got a nephew," I tell my sister when I call her not much later.

She cries; so do I.

"Is he beautiful?" she asks.

I look at the swollen, angry head on my chest, eyes tightly closed, mouth wide open.

"I have no idea," I say. "I can't see properly."

When my daughter comes home later that afternoon, my partner and I make sure neither of us is holding her little brother. That's better, I've read on a parenting website, if we want to prevent jealousy.

Instead, he's lying on his back in the crib. Tiny eyes closed, tiny arms up, total surrender. Someone has dressed him in a tiny vest and tiny trousers, with a tiny hat on top, but that can't hide the fact that he seems to have come from another planet, a different species. He's not yet entirely human, not yet entirely ours.

The three of us bend down over the little sleeping intruder. My partner and I observe our daughter. How she looks at him, her prolonged, silent fascination. Then she turns to me and asks me to lift my shirt. She feels my slack but still rounded belly, a belly that hasn't yet realized it's empty now. She nods in satisfaction.

"Yep," she says, "your belly's gone."

In the days that follow we scrutinize her for signs of jealousy, of a traumatic dethronement, of the start of that "permanent estrangement" Freud talked about.

There's the time she wets herself on the sofa while I'm feeding her little brother.

There's the time in the playground: I thought he might sleep a bit longer, but he wakes up and cries for milk. I interrupt our game to give him some, to which she responds by hanging from my hair, all twenty-six pounds of her.

But the outbursts of rage, the sleep problems, the wild envy—we're ready for them, but they fail to material-ize. This doesn't change in the weeks that follow, weeks in which it must dawn on her that the baby isn't going to go away. That he'll stay, whether we really need him or not.

○

It's not until autumn, when the first feverish days of my son's existence are far behind us, the sleepless nights have died down a little, and my daughter still hasn't turned on us, that I begin to question the vision I had before his arrival. Maybe jealousy isn't as universal and inevitable as I feared—or in any case, for our family, not nearly so devastating.

Maybe the last word on the matter has yet to be said.

In the afternoons, when my daughter is at daycare, my son asleep in the crib, I go back online. This time I ignore the parenting forums with their lists of precautions and visit the more serious regions of the internet—databases of academic articles, university research pages. As it turns out, in the past four decades (more or less from the moment that two became the norm) a growing num-ber of psychologists, anthropologists, and developmental psychologists have discovered that sibling relationships are worth investigating.

Brothers and sisters are as ancient as humanity, of course, and most social sciences have existed since the nineteenth century, so forty years really isn't very long at all. Especially if you consider that around 80 to 90 percent of the world's population has at least one sibling, and that siblings, when they are little, often spend more time with each other than with anyone else.[1]

But academia was so preoccupied with the influence of parents on their children that the rest of the family was long overlooked.[2] Whenever siblings did feature in psychological theory, they did so either as an afterthought or as the cause of trouble—of envy, dethronement, the stuff of nightmares.

Perhaps it was the desire for a new take, a fresh look, that motivated a new generation of psychologists to more rigorously test what had, meanwhile, become generally accepted truths. They sought to find out whether parents really were all-important in a child's life, or whether other family members might matter too; and they didn't feel comfortable taking the destructive nature of sibling rivalry at face value. Enthusiasm about Sigmund Freud's ideas began to wane in the 1970s; this too might have allowed for a more encompassing vision to arise. Either way, there is now a small but growing field that one might call "sibling science."

The findings of these researchers have been reported in academic journals and textbooks, in a language I had not previously connected with parenthood. I learn, for instance, about "parental resource dilution" when a family has more than one child; the way parents "invest" in their progeny; and the "outcomes" of those investments.

But what I *do* recognize is the longing to grasp by the wings the ways in which our choices affect our children, to pin them down and place them under a magnifying glass. Because the insight you stand to gain seems to offer certainty, the promise of predictability, and hence control.

And perhaps also, because I somehow believe in the possibility, if I do my very best to understand it all, of getting it right as a parent.

It was a British developmental psychologist named Judy Dunn who, at the end of the 1970s, was one of the first to make sibling relationships the focus of her research. She began with the much-feared origin of trouble: the arrival of a second child.

Dunn approached forty-one families who had a second child on the way, visiting them just before the birth and several times afterward and filling notebooks with her observations. One of the things that most stood out for her was that firstborn children suddenly had to deal with a good deal less attention from their parents—and in particular with less positive, patient, and sympathetic attention.[3] In addition to a little brother or sister, elder children also had to withstand more rebukes and fewer touchy-feely moments.

Tell me about it, I think when I read Dunn's findings. In the early days and weeks of my son's existence, one image kept coming back to me. It was the image of a bird's nest, wide-open chicks' beaks sticking out, harassed father and mother bird frantically flying back and forth to fill their little mouths.

My daughter and son each had their own needs, and their rhythms were completely out of sync. The time went tortuously slowly, and yet there never seemed to be enough of it: I found myself in a constant hurry, in search of moments I could steal from the baby to give to his sister and vice versa.

○

The scene that has stayed with me the most from those early weeks plays out on a muggy day in early autumn. I'm dizzy with sleep deprivation and feverish from incipient mastitis, my son is crying on the back seat, and my daughter is refusing to get into her car seat.

A couple of weeks earlier, I know for certain, I would have been better rested and calmer, more understanding. I would have been more tolerant of the procrastination. But not today. She screams, struggles, and with greater force than is warranted, I shove her into her car seat. It's not inconceivable that I squeeze her little arm just a little too long.

Shame follows immediately. (It's an emotion that, like guilt, may well be an inherent part of parenthood, a state that demands sacrifices we're not always prepared to make—and not only awakens in us an unprecedented capacity for love and care, but also confronts us time and again with the most impatient, most curmudgeonly and irascible side of ourselves.)

○

For most children, Dunn writes, the arrival of a second child is a big transition—in part due to that sudden reduction in parental attention. That transition, like other big changes, can be stressful, and in response to that stress young children may develop sleep problems and tantrums.[4] They can turn whiny or anxious, or exhibit regressive behavior—suddenly go back to crawling or wetting the bed, for example, the kinds of behavior that the parenting websites warn of as well.

Such regressions can be explained in various ways, I read in a book by the Dutch child psychiatrist Frits Boer, who worked with Dunn in the 1990s. The simplest explanation is that the transition just takes a great deal of energy—adults, too, "behave more childishly" when they're tired, as Boer observes.

According to a different, more biological explanation, the regression is intended to retain parental attention: I'm not as independent as I look, says the toddler who suddenly goes back to babbling like a baby; don't forget about me!

The third explanation, which I love the most, holds that "the eldest child, by imitating the youngest, can better identify with the youngest." There's no exhaustion or jealousy at the root of it, just an attempt at identification: "This way," Boer writes, "it's easier for him to give the youngest child a place in his emotional life."[5]

Whichever explanation is right—and it seems likely each of them is, in a way, right—they're all more layered and nuanced than the doom-and-gloom scenarios raised by the theorists of the nineteenth century. Those scenarios, after all, had been heavy on dethronement, all-consuming jealousy, and trauma that lasted a lifetime. The light cast by modern-day sibling scientists is much more gentle, and hopeful too.

Because, what's more, Dunn saw in her research that far from all children were plagued by sleep problems, tantrums, or regression. In the majority of cases, such issues were temporary or never arose at all. The idea that the arrival of a second child necessarily means the irreparable dethronement of the first, that hate and envy toward the little invader are all-important, turns out to be primarily just that: an idea.[6]

○

Another memory from the beginning. We're sitting in the window seat, my son and daughter and I; he's lying on my thighs, where his entire being fits.

He's asleep.

She's sitting next to me; outside, driving rain colors the water in the canal a strange shade of yellow. Both of us are gazing at her little brother. Then she says, with the intonation of surprised satisfaction she must have picked up from visitors in the past few days, "He's really *dark*, isn't he?"

It's as if the arrival of the second child hasn't so much dethroned her as catapulted her into a different world with which to identify herself: the world of grown-ups tasked with caring for the baby, examining and categorizing him.

○

Most children are between two and three years old when a little sibling comes along. Developmentally, that's precisely the moment when they tend to be at their most aggressive, least obedient, and most demanding.[7] In order to find out what the arrival of a second child does to a firstborn who is in the tantrum phase anyway, ideally you would study that child for a while beforehand, and for a good while afterward.

That's precisely what Brenda Volling of the University of Michigan has been doing for several years now. She's the director of the Family Transitions Study, in which 241 families are followed to map out how a first child reacts to the birth of a second, how that reaction influences the relationship between the two children, and how families adjust to the new situation.

As far as I can tell, it's the most extensive empirical study so far of the arrival of a second child—and of what Volling calls the "transition to siblinghood." But even if 241 families is a big group for one research team, it's very small for humanity, and the findings aren't necessarily representative of *all* families.[8] Nevertheless, I find the conclusion of her research reassuring: when it comes to the claim that the arrival of a sibling causes children life-long trauma, Volling found no evidence at all. The vast majority of children in the study were doing pretty much fine beforehand, and although some did exhibit certain behavioral problems around the birth of their brother or sister—aggression, in particular, could increase substantially—most of them were back to their old selves after four months.

Four months! On the scale of a human lifetime, that's nothing.

It's also worth noting that, for some children, emotional and behavioral problems actually *decreased*, probably due to the simple fact that they got older. Like Judy Dunn, Volling concludes that all-consuming jealousy is rare, if it exists at all.

It occurs to me that what's true of drugs and medicine might be true of jealousy as well: it all comes down to dosage. In small quantities it's not that bad, and in the absence of other cause for concern, it's nothing to be scared of.

But the shadow cast by Freud, with his focus on pathological developments, still influences our ideas about the transition to siblinghood, Brenda Volling writes in a 2017 monograph. The titles of the parenting books I acquired in the run-up to the arrival of our second child say it all. The result, Volling observes, is that many parents worry about what they're doing to their firstborn and that mothers often approach the arrival of a second child with trepidation. Which is a shame, since most children are a good deal more resilient than we think.[9]

I can see it in my daughter. The way she adapts to the new situation, the interrupted mealtimes, the tired parents, the feeding of the baby, which always takes priority over everything else. The way she sometimes grumbles, but is always quick to bounce back. The way she's so satisfied with the solution I've picked up from one of the books: when you need to feed the baby, just put your toddler in front of the TV.

It's a compromise, but it works.

Her Netflix addiction is off to a flying start.

I see how happy she is with the little gifts visitors bring her—they probably read that recommendation somewhere too. A couple of weeks earlier I'd mentioned to friends that no, we did not have a box full of pink dressing-up clothes—so stereotypical!—and lo and behold, her first princess dress arrives, a synthetic pink tulle creation, complete with shocking-pink plastic earrings, a magic wand, and a crown.

Dressed up as an explosion of pixie dust, she bends over her brother as he sleeps on the sofa or in the crib, strokes his head, says he's sweet, when visitors ask, and then continues with her game.

I can see my daughter's ability to adapt and to cope, but evidently I was unable to *fore*see it.

Perhaps that's because I was navigating with my own experience, my own childhood for a compass. And in doing so, I managed to reduce all the possible reasons why my sister and I fought so fiercely all those years—from clashing aspirations and characters to straightforward irritations—to one single cause: jealousy. A hundred and fifty years of parental advice, from Sigmund Freud to *Siblings Without Rivalry*, made no attempt to dissuade me of that explanation.

It's also possible, it occurs to me after reading Volling's work, that the parental sense of responsibility is in fact predicated upon vulnerable children—be they first- or second-born. Or rather, upon the *idea* that children are vulnerable, anything but resilient. And that that notion, which arises, of course, from fear, not only determines how you treat your children but also what you expect of them.

At the beginning of this century, an international band of psychologists published an article titled "Bad Is Stronger Than Good." Having done the rounds of the psychological literature, the authors concluded that a lot more had been written on negative psychological events, states, and development than on what might work out *well* in a person's life.

From an evolutionary perspective, the finding was easy to explain: in order to survive, it's more important to be alert to danger than to find out how to become even happier. Better to remember that you need to jump away when a car rushes headlong toward you than that it can feel great to take a few deep breaths as soon as you get outside on an early spring day.

That's why negative events, such as losing friends or money or being criticized, affect most people more than making friends, winning money, or receiving compliments, as experiment after experiment has shown.[10] Bad has a bigger impact on us than good.

That's why psychologists have long been more interested in the issues that upset us than the things that make our lives worth living. (Although the new research area of "positive psychology" has begun to change that.) That may also be why many parents expecting a second child focus most on what might go wrong between the first and the second. And why scary scenarios on dethronement and jealousy, originating in the nineteenth century, still make more of an impression on our views than the more nuanced findings of recent researchers.

And that's probably also why I read *There's Going to Be a Baby* so many times to my daughter. To prepare her for an event whose consequences no one could predict, but for which I expected the worst, just to be on the safe side.

3

Again, again

On the joy of repetition and
the wonder of reminiscence

My notes begin when my son is five weeks old. They're
less detailed and methodical than Charles Darwin's observations of William, but there are plenty of them. And
just like Darwin, I notice when I leaf back through them
months later, I regularly mention facial expressions.

In my first entry, my father observes that his grandson
"has a look just like Harrison Ford."

A couple of days later, I pick up my son from his cradle at half past five in the morning; for the first time, he
doesn't want to feed straightaway but looks around—
"smiling," I've added.

That same week I've noted that my partner thinks our
son looks "angry," while I would classify his expression
more as "worried."

(Evidently I have the presence of mind to note that

the fact that we each read something different into his expression probably says more about us than about our son.)

Besides his expressions, in the early days I mainly observe how my son fills his time and mine. I describe hours slept and hours spent awake, fits of crying calmed or endured, walking routes completed or abandoned prematurely.

Later I write about his first shriek of laughter and what occasioned it. I record when he starts dribbling and report on its sudden disappearance. His first day at daycare is noted, as is the end of breastfeeding—which leaves me simultaneously relieved and sad, while apparently having hardly any effect on him at all.

When he's half a year old I try to put his clumsy manner of waving into words, the way he uses his upper arm instead of his forearm. I write that he manages to roll from his back to his front but not yet the other way, note the fascinated gaze with which he watches his sister.

His first steps.

His first words.

The notes don't tell a story. They're not systematic, not in search of bigger lines or underlying patterns. That's not the point here: where Darwin's motivation for note-taking was scientific, mine is sentimental.

I started it to get a grip on time.

To prevent myself from rapidly forgetting everything that's happening now.

There's no such thing from my daughter's early years,

no notes. I barely wrote anything down with her, aside from a couple of sporadic, hastily typed reports and lists of early utterances. I didn't realize then how little of it would stick, wasn't conscious of the fleeting nature of her baby phase and the fallibility of my memory. I was in the midst of it all and could hardly imagine that it would ever pass.

This time I want to arm myself against forgetfulness. And this, this changed consciousness, is one way in which the second time is different from the first, in which repetition differs from the first time.

○

When my son turns one, he becomes addicted to a thick board picture book of nursery rhymes. The second spread shows a colorful picture of two fish looking at each other, one orange and alert, the other blue and displaying an expression of pure horror. My son points at the illustration, hums, and I sing the accompanying Dutch rhyme about a fish who, like most fish, can't speak and spends his days swimming around and around in a bowl.

I don't know if it's the tormented blue fish on the left-hand page that causes the song to strike me as so cruel and depressing. Perhaps it's the combination of image and lyrics that does it, especially the ruthlessness of the last phrase, "Just turn around": the command comes across as a sort of punishment for the poor fish's speech impediment.

When, as a child, I had goldfish for a while, someone

told me that these creatures have a short-term memory of only a few seconds. So it wasn't sad, their having such a small tank to swim endlessly up and down in, because they perceived time differently from us. They lived in a continuous "now," everything was always new for them, every time the first time.

When I've finished singing, my son looks at me in delight. "Again," he says, "again."

I sing it again. The second, third, and fourth times he seems to like it just as much as the first, as if the song is new to him every time. Or perhaps the rerun simply pleases him as much as the premiere. More so, even, because it's preceded by anticipation.

It was around my daughter's first birthday that I began to long for repetition. I wanted to feel a baby moving inside a growing belly again. I wanted to hold a tiny, warm body again, a torso on my chest and a little head in my palm. The security, the devotion, the stunning combination of responsibility and vulnerability—I wanted all of that again.

My longing was way ahead of my partner's. Why, he wondered, would we put ourselves once more through the sleep deprivation, the shredded nights, the fuss and the hassle? Why would we disrupt a situation that worked and was good, the balance we'd achieved? And where would we live and what about climate change? Every day brought new alarming newspaper reports on sea levels rising, resources running out, overconsumption and over-population.

But I was like the main character in Jessie Greengrass's novel *Sight*, a mother who wants to do it again, in spite of it all. Partly because she wants "an ally" for her daughter. But mainly because she "cannot bear the thought of never holding another sleeping baby, the agony of their eyelids, their mouths, their skin."[1] I couldn't understand why my partner saw things differently.

So I responded to his hesitation with sadness, with premature disappointment, like a child afraid of missing out on a fiercely desired toy. The prospect of a possible rejection only made me all the greedier.

Even then, I couldn't really have thought the second time would work out precisely the same as the first. But my expectations as to how it would be were based on how it went with my daughter: it was that experience I wanted to repeat.

Again, I thought, *again*.

○

I knew what I longed for, and at the same time I didn't know that at all. I had no idea, after all, what this specific form of repetition would entail, didn't know what it meant to have a child when you already have one.

For decades, social scientists have taken pleasure in comparing happiness levels among parents with those of nonparents—and subsequently, almost without exception, concluding that having children doesn't make people happier, and in some cases even makes people *un*happier than a childless existence.[2]

Some studies are nuanced enough to break parent-hood down into two sides: it produces meaningful, joyful, and fulfilling experiences, but also a great deal of frustration, boredom, and exhaustion.[3] (And perhaps one doesn't exist without the other; if someone can fulfill you, writes British psychoanalyst Adam Phillips in his essay "On Frustration," then they can frustrate you as well—simply by withholding that which you desire from them.[4])

In any case, according to these studies, the arrival of a second child doesn't usually increase happiness. An American meta-analysis of parenthood and relationship quality found that the more children a couple has, the less satisfied the partners are with their marriage.[5] Two demographers who examined happiness levels among parents in as many as eighty-six countries concluded that each additional child made their parents a little less happy.[6]

It does depend *when* you ask parents how happy they are.[7] A study of Germans and Brits, for example, showed that parents, and particularly mothers, were extra happy around the birth of their first child. That peak was temporary, though: in time, parents were back to prepregnancy levels.

Statistics Netherlands (CBS) also reports that Dutch people are happiest in the year they have their first child. The spike in happiness begins *before* the baby is born: looking forward to it alone creates the effect—the expectation, the anticipation, the prospect.[8] What is also apparent from the Statistics Netherlands data is that a similar increase in happiness is absent when it comes to a second or third pregnancy and birth.

That might have been down to the chosen research method, as in the study of Germans and Brits a happiness spike *was* observed the second time around.[9] It was far less intense, though; parents were approximately half as happy around the birth of their second child as they were around the birth of their first.[10] After that, the effect rather wore off—a third child brought no peak in happiness whatsoever.

○

Me, I was euphoric when my son arrived. High from the hormones and lack of sleep and the heat but also from a strange sort of elation.

It was an elation that might collapse into gloom at any moment, and which perhaps felt more intense because of that. Maybe it wasn't rapture so much as joy: that "strange admixture of terror, pain and delight," as Zadie Smith aptly describes it in her essay on the matter.[11]

The sensation wasn't even that different from how I'd felt after the first birth, though my delight was rather more measured this time. Because besides a newborn son, I now also had a daughter. A daughter about whom, rightly or wrongly, I was worried, and for whom it was best, I'd read somewhere, if her life remained, as far as possible, as it had been.

So although everything was completely different, we shouldn't permit too much to change. That automatically put a damper on my ecstasy, set boundaries for my joy, formed a considerable counterweight.

Mikko Myrskylä, lead researcher of that study of new German and British parents, offered another explanation for the reduced spike in happiness around the arrival of a second child. Perhaps, he said in a university press release, the decline had to do with the fact that "the experience of parenthood" had become "less novel and exciting."[12]

Or to put it another way, because repetition takes away the shine.

His remark makes me think of what happens when you take ecstasy: how after the first high you can take another hit, but the second wave of euphoria is always a watered-down version of the first. The extra dose of happiness therefore comes with a slight sense of disappointment.

I think, too, of the impression first times can make in general. I remember in detail the first time I rode a horse, fell in love, my first campfire to top off a night out. I remember the first time a boy placed my hand on his heart so I could feel how it was beating, the smell of 183rd Street when I first arrived in New York City, the epiphany when I first read Joan Didion.

I can't visualize second, third, fourth times as sharply. The memories have become intermingled; they now refer to archetypes rather than separate experiences.

In *Felt Time: The Science of How We Experience Time* by the psychologist Marc Wittmann, I read that new experiences require more attention, activate the brain more forcefully, and are better recorded in memory than experiences that resemble what you already know.[13] From an evolutionary perspective, it makes sense that the brain works this way: in order to survive, the most important thing is to notice the novel and the unfamiliar and draw lessons from it. Repeatedly being amazed about how a certain tree filters the sunlight at a particular time of day is rather less essential.

Could it be this psychological mechanism that makes most of us so partial to first times, so keen to seek out new experiences and tell each other stories about the first time we kissed someone, or saw the mountains, or went on an airplane? Is it this that causes our tendency to prize youthful freedom over the experience that comes with age, and leads us collectively to celebrate innovation and originality? That allows us to grant one another "second chances," but otherwise largely causes us to associate "the second" with something lesser?

I'm hardly aware of any praise of repetition; I know few odes to recognition, barely any celebrations of routine.

○

It wasn't the same, having a child for the second time. Of course it wasn't the same: *I* wasn't the same. I'd already done it once. For that reason, the most important factor that characterized the first pregnancy and birth was absent—namely being overwhelmed by a completely new experience.

There was something else instead: anticipation. I knew roughly how my body would behave during pregnancy. How tired I would be, how scatterbrained. How phenomenally massive my breasts would become, how round my belly; how I would bruise more easily and my skin would be even more sensitive to the sun than usual.

Those expectations were more or less met: I was just as tired and absent-minded; the changes in my body were fairly similar, with some subtle differences here and there (breasts slightly smaller, belly—how was it possible?—slightly rounder still).

Had the shine worn off, the second time? If anything, something had been added: expectation based on previous experience. There was amazement again, certainly. It remains a simultaneously fascinating and terrifying fact, the unimaginable cell division in your uterus resulting in a baby. The fact that it all works, without you having to do anything for it, without even understanding it.

But it was an amazement I saw coming—I recognized it.

I knew the birth would be different. Giving birth is easier the second time around, the books assured me, as did the midwives and the mothers who'd been there.

It was sweltering, the day the contractions came on, the air utterly stifling. When my daughter was born, my foremost feeling had been one of indignation—"Millions of years of evolution," I'd bellowed between contractions, "and still we're stuck with such a terrible system!"

This time I greeted the pain with resignation, like you would a visitor who had once behaved unacceptably but who couldn't be turned away now.

Time went slower and slower over the course of that night, until it seemed to elapse only to the rhythm of the pain.

What I remember is that I longed for a number of completely incompatible things. I wished the end would come quickly, that time would pass rapidly—and with the time, the pain. I also wished I could stop time, pause it indefinitely. So that I could rest for a moment, but also to stretch out this experience of giving birth a while longer. Because this would probably be the last time I experienced it. And later I wanted something else entirely: when the midwife had arrived and my daughter had left, I wished I could turn the time right back.

Outside, the day was cautiously dawning by then, and suddenly I saw clearly what we'd brought upon ourselves. I saw that there was about to be a second child, a fourth family member. An infant asking for milk every two hours, who needed cleaning, rocking, figuring out. That in time that infant would become a laughing baby and then a talking toddler, and from there: a small child in preschool, a serious eleven-year-old, a child leaving home, on holiday, to work or to school. And then, who knew, a young guy in love, a father perhaps, a wrinkled old man with unfulfilled longings and regrets.

I was so exhausted by the prospect, by all the steps between now and the end, and by my role in it all, that I wanted to go back, undo his arrival. Too late, of course, much too late: he was already on his way out.

With my daughter, I can remember precisely the first time I saw her. Her round, red little head, the tormented yet resigned gaze in her eyes.

I couldn't see my son very well when he was on my chest, when my sister asked over the phone if he was beautiful.

But I could hear him well enough. He screamed, deafeningly, and a lot longer than his sister had done. Longer, too, than seemed warranted. The midwife didn't appear to notice anything out of the ordinary, nor did the maternity assistant or my partner. They quietly did what was required of them—testing reflexes, checking the damage, dressing, tidying up, calling relatives.

I tried to calm my son, gently patted his naked back, mumbled "oh" and "ah" and "come on" and "sorry," but he continued to scream. I began to fear I wouldn't manage to quiet him, that his rage and sadness came from somewhere very deep down. That he didn't really want to be here, that he somehow knew what I'd wished for just a couple of hours previously.

I tried to attract the attention of the other adults, my partner and the cheerful midwife and her assistant, wanted to ask them what was wrong, what I should do, but I couldn't make myself heard over his bellowing.

Suddenly, without any clear reason, he was quiet. And then, silent.

○

My sister: Is he beautiful?
   Me: I have no idea. I can't see properly.

○

It's often said that you forget the pain of birth so that you can do it all again. That the same goes for the first sleepless weeks and months with a baby: that "nature" ensures we can no longer clearly recall these experiences once they are behind us. Because there would be no second children born at all if we could remember precisely how it was the first time.

That might explain why, after the birth of my daughter, I hardly made any notes, and only began to do so with my son when he was several weeks old. That in those notes I mainly focused on details and stand-alone observations—facial expressions, times, routes—much more than on how it *felt*, how overwhelming and contradictory it all was.

And it might explain why, when the second hadn't yet been born, I mainly imagined a warm, soft, adorable newborn—not, for instance, the oppressive feeling of a baby who can't be calmed, or the assault on body and mind that such a baby brings along with it; the body trying to find its way back to its original form, without ever fully getting there; the mind that feels simultaneously colonized and depopulated—two contradictory phenomena, strangely enough with the same effect.

"I often think," writes Rachel Cusk in her book *A Life's Work*, "that people wouldn't have children if they knew what it was like, and I wonder whether as a gender we contain a Darwinian stop upon our powers of expression, our ability to render the truth of this subject."[14]

Could it be that evolution imposes a stop on us mothers, a blockade whereby we're unable to describe parenthood to the uninitiated?

Perhaps that stop, if it exists, isn't so different from our capacity to forget.

My sister says I still share very little with her. The days we used to fight over toys or clothes are long gone, but still, she says, I keep my emotions and experiences to myself.

She mentions her own motherhood as an example—her daughter, my niece, was born after my first child and before my second.

"I thought it would bring us closer together," she tells me one Saturday that we spend at a pavement café, for once not surrounded or distracted by our children. "I was going to experience something you had already been through, something big and momentous, something that from then on we'd have in common."

But when she asked me how certain things had been for me—how much energy I had in the fifth month of pregnancy, what my daughter's sleep pattern was like in the early weeks, how often she fed when she was a couple of months old—I only gave her vague answers.

"You'd forgotten everything," my sister says.

She sounds surprised, not to mention a little accusatory. But perhaps, I think as I listen to her, my inability to give her the details she was asking for had to do with the fact that many of her questions weren't about the big, gripping issues.

They weren't about what I thought and felt when I saw my daughter for the first time, but about how our days looked when she had already been here for a little while.

Not about the first time she slept through the night, but about the course of the many broken nights that preceded it.

Not about the wonder, but about what came after: the endless repetition, the routine.

○

I speak to a neuropsychologist who specializes in time perception. We talk about children and memory. When experiences are new, he says, you make lots of new memories. If an experience is already familiar, you remember less about it. Routine crushes memories—or rather, it prevents them ever being made.

Routine also happens to be one of the main characteristics of new parenthood: the same round of playground and supermarket every time, the same tune at daycare every day, that one song that has to be sung in exactly the same way every evening. Again, again: it's what children want and so it's what new parents do, day in, day out, whether they want to or not.

"This new life laid down in daily patterns" is how the young mother in *Sight* characterizes it: "a structure ossified by repetition until I could barely remember what it had been like before."[15]

(A study that followed approximately five hundred Swedish women until five years after the birth of their first child showed that mothers who scored high on what was called the "personality monotony avoidance scale" were less likely to have a second child than those who scored lower. A high score on the scale indicates the tendency to seek out new experiences. The fact that these very experience-oriented women were less keen to have a second child, the researchers wrote, might be because "life with children is seen as an existence with set routines." This made motherhood "unappealing" to that group.[16])

With a second child, the neuropsychologist speculates, you might get into a routine even more quickly than with a first. The experience is, after all, already more or less familiar, and there is less of a sense of inundation. In that case, you might forget even more the second time than you did the first.

"Do you have fewer memories of the second than of the first?" he wants to know.

I probe my memory. It's true that the second time feels less like embarking on a voyage of discovery in a wild, foreign country, that there are some things I saw coming—his first laugh, his first attempt to shuffle forward, his first fit of rage. In that sense, the surprise is smaller. What for him is the first time, for me is repetition—at least in part.

Nevertheless, I don't believe I've retained fewer memories, or no fewer than with his sister, about whom I've also forgotten a great deal—after all, that was the whole reason I decided to make notes the second time around.

There's something else going on, I tell the neuropsychologist, when it comes to my memories of my first and second child. They're beginning to *intermingle*.

The nocturnal feeds in the blue glow of Twitter's endless scroll, for example—I can visualize them easily, but it's no longer clear which baby I'm holding in that moment.

A newborn baby in a sling, on a walk along the canal, the feeling of kicking feet against my still-soft belly—it happened once in winter and once in summer, but in my memory it all happens on the same neutral, slightly cloudy day that could feature in any season.

My partner says he's forgotten at which birth he got to cut the umbilical cord—the first or the second. (Wasn't it both?) As far as he retains memories of a specific birth, he can distinguish by my position on the sofa: left when our daughter was born, right when our son came along. But when it comes to cord-cutting, he doesn't have that image to hand.

Another factor of repetition, of the second time, is that things I hadn't thought about again after the first time have come back to me.

The pain of giving birth—*oh, yes, that's how it felt*.

The baby who unfurled a little more by the hour after the birth, looked less and less like a generic newborn and more and more like itself: *oh, yes*.

The newborn repeatedly needing to feed, my body making it possible, the attempts, doomed to fail, at discerning a rhythm to him: I'd forgotten; now I was reminded.

The sinking feeling on realizing his dependence, his vulnerability, accompanied by the elation because he was there, because it had worked out: *oh, yes, that's how it was*.

I put music on and my son starts to dance, immersed in himself; he stares ahead, beats on an imaginary instrument, still too uncoordinated to call it air drums, and wobbles his head. I look at him, and suddenly it comes back to me: his sister danced in precisely the same manner, two years earlier and to different music, but with that same absorption.

Would I ever have thought of that again, if he hadn't just done it?

He's starting to talk, slowly but surely, and his first words remind me of hers.

I take a photo, and his gaze reminds me of a previous photo, one I took of his sister.

I scroll through my telephone searching for the image, see the second growing younger and disappearing, so that only the first remains, a couple of years younger and with a gaze that certainly resembles that of her little brother now.

Memory experts say that memories change a little each time you retrieve them—because you've changed a bit yourself. Memories aren't fixed, but re-created time and again, adjusted to the aim they serve at that moment.

In that sense, writes psychological historian Douwe Draaisma, memories are "reconstructions rather than recapitulations of our experiences." And those reconstructions are not only influenced by "who we once were but by who we have become . . . by the time in which memories are called to mind."[17] I remember my daughter *because* my son repeats something she did; I remember the behavior or facial expression precisely in the way that makes it fit.

Every memory is unique, a one-off. The same goes for repetition, I suppose now, for what happens when you experience things again. Every repetition is a new experience in itself: the expectations you have, which sometimes are and sometimes aren't fulfilled, are new. The recognition is new. The memories that become entangled, that melt together or lead to one another: they're all new.

And *he's* new.

Of course, a lot of what's now happening, I'm experiencing for the second time—but it's the first time I've been through it with *him*. And he's anything but a repetition of his sister, anything but a copy.

He's completely himself, a unique human being.

Another new feature with the second child: how my daughter, amazed and careful, takes her newborn little brother onto her lap.

How, a couple of months later, he laughs at her for the first time.

How, in short, it's not only a second child that has been added to our family: a new relationship has begun as well, a relationship between brother and sister. How this has been the birth of hundreds of new reasons for fear, tenderness, and surprise.

And at least as many reasons to wonder what it means to *them*, that there's two of them now.

4

A fly buzzing around my ear

On siblings and only children

I ask my sister about her memories of our childhood. She has three ready to go.

In the first, we're fighting over a particular cup: it's hers; I want it. I tell her that I recently caught a spider in it, and my sister, arachnophobe that she is, relinquishes it immediately. She never dared drink from it again.

The second memory is of a white wicker doll's stroller that my sister thought was mine—that's what I had told her. Only recently did she discover, leafing through old photo albums, that *she* was the one who had received it as a gift.

And the third memory is about an occasion on which I—quite exceptionally—gave her permission to play with me. I'd set up a museum in my bedroom and allowed my sister to visit. The entrance fee was a guilder. She must have come along at least ten times, obediently buying a ticket every time.

She tells me the stories on a Friday night at the end of winter. We're sitting at the big wooden table in her living room, drinking a type of tea my mother always makes. Her daughter is in bed but not yet asleep; over the baby monitor we can hear her processing the day out loud, her high voice against a background of rustling radio waves.

It's shortly before my niece is to turn two. Whether there'll be a second, my sister doesn't yet know. It strikes her as exhausting, two children—she points to the bags under my eyes and my pale face. I don't dare ask to what extent her memories, which paint a less than rosy picture of life with an elder sister, play a part in her hesitation.

But the alternative is equally unappealing, she says: "Then we'll end up with an only child."[1]

○

At the foundation of my sister's claim lies a broadly shared conviction. Namely, the conviction that you're better off with a sibling than without one. The nineteenth-century US psychologist G. Stanley Hall, for example, once noted that being an only child is "a disease in itself."

The general thinking on only children didn't improve much after that statement. The Austrian pediatrician Karl König, for instance, observed halfway through the last century that an only child was "often peculiar in his behavior and usually rather immature in his social conduct." He added that it was "not too difficult to understand the special position of such a lonely bird."[2]

And regarding China, the only country in the world where, for a couple of horrifying decades, the "standard family" imposed by the government was a one-child family, it was soon said that the new generation suffered from "little emperor syndrome."

The clichés regarding only children appear to be even more firmly rooted in our collective consciousness than stories about first children, dethroned and traumatized by the arrival of a second.[3]

My daughter was ten months old when my father-in-law asked me if we'd have a second child. I said I didn't know, she'd only just arrived, we'd have to see.

"It would be sad for her, though," he said, "to be on her own." He'd worked in education for forty years and could pick them out at a glance, the only children: egocentric, spoiled, a bit out of touch.

It struck me as a tactless remark—there was a chance, after all, that our first would remain our only child. But I was tired, as I have been more or less the entire time the past five years. So I mumbled something noncommittal, then held my tongue.

Even after it had become clear that our daughter wouldn't be an only child, his remark remained with me. I began to suspect that if we were having the second "for the first," it was as much of an incantation as a gift. That not only do we want to *give* our children something; we want to protect them from something as well.

Only now that my son is here do I wonder how rational all that is.

Sometimes it seems as though the social sciences are in the business of confirming, with great fanfare, what everyone already knew. But sometimes they succeed in overturning a deep-rooted conviction—and such is the case with the study of only children and the ways in which they may or may not differ from those who grow up with siblings.

According to a meta-analysis from 1986, reviewing the research that had been conducted on only children in the previous half century, the cognitive, emotional, and social development of singletons was hardly distinguishable from that of eldest children and children from small families.[4] This has remained the conclusion of research conducted in the decades since: at most, only children differ in being, on average, slightly more motivated at school and college. They apparently also have a higher "sense of self-esteem," I read in the book on sibling relationships by the child psychiatrist Frits Boer.[5]

There are always exceptions, of course. But for the assumptions that only children are less sociable, more spoiled, less smart, or more egocentric than those whose parents have given them siblings, scientists effectively find no evidence.[6]

Perhaps only children have long known this, and it's just brothers and sisters and their parents who are confused. The one thing only children *do* struggle with, the developmental psychologist Sheila van Berkel of Leiden University once told me, is the prejudice around being an only child.

Perhaps we've mistaken the norm for what is good—come to see the fact that only children are the exception as evidence of their disadvantage.

(Aside from all that, according to some studies, the *parents* of only children are the happiest of all: they get the benefits of being a parent without the downsides of having multiple children—such as having to divide their time and attention, handling the increased financial pressure, battling the extra burdens on their energy, and having to intervene in arguments.[7])

I listen to my sister's childhood memories and her hesitations over whether to have a second child. I think of how my mother had her second child for her first—and of how ungratefully her first child received that gift, how carelessly I treated my sister for so many years. So far, my daughter is shaping up to be a better custodian of her little brother. But that doesn't change the fact that she's had to trade something in for him—even if it was just a large quantity of patient, sympathetic parental attention and the *illusion*, at least, that we had all the time in the world for her.

So the question remains: when we give our firstborns

a little brother or sister, what exactly are we giving them? What do we know about the relationship between siblings, about what our children stand to gain—or lose— from each other?

○

When the British developmental psychologist Judy Dunn began her research on sibling relationships forty years ago, she studied not only families around the arrival of a second baby, but also the interaction between siblings who were a little older.

She regularly saw brothers and sisters who exhibited friendly, cooperative, and helpful behavior. They played together and comforted each other easily, Dunn explained, because they knew each other and each other's world so well.

But it was precisely that knowledge and regular time together, she added, that meant "that siblings are particularly well placed to tease, annoy, and compete," as well— almost 30 percent of interactions between brothers and sisters in an early study consisted of fighting.[8]

It can't have been particularly shocking news in the 1970s and 1980s that sibling relationships could be both heartwarmingly sweet and dreadfully irritating. Elsewhere in the animal kingdom, too, brothers and sisters beat each other up just as often as they help each other out, I read in *A Natural History of Families* by US behavioral ecologist Scott Forbes.

Forbes writes with evident glee about baby eagles that haven't even fully hatched before they're crushed by their elder sibling, and tiger sharks that go at one another *in the womb.*

All this, he adds, can be neatly explained from an evolutionary perspective. Since siblings on average have half their genetic makeup in common, they benefit from each other's reproductive success—hence their helping, supporting, and protecting each other where possible. At the same time, they compete for attention, food, and other parental resources, so they're rivals as well.[9]

Forbes's book roams around our house for weeks, moving from the kitchen table to the windowsill to the bookcase and back. Sometimes I read excerpts aloud to my partner: I regale him with tales of ants who eat their little siblings in times of famine, of the relentlessness of cuckoo chicks.

Meanwhile, things are proceeding rather more peacefully in our own nest.

We watch my son climb into the back compartment of the tricycle my daughter is on.

"Taxi!" my daughter shouts, as she begins to pedal. Her passenger crows with pleasure.

Where evolutionary biologists stop, Dunn and other sibling scientists keep going. They attempt to map out how we're shaped by the humdrum, nonpathological interactions between brothers and sisters—the everyday scrapping and bickering, play and care, collusion and support.

For this purpose they observe families, conduct

surveys, let mathematical formulae loose on data sets great and small. They search for patterns and averages, for rules and associations.

Their research demonstrates that siblings do influence one another's cognitive, emotional, and moral development. And often that influence is positive: there is some substance to the intuition of many parents that having a sibling can be beneficial.

For example, in an overview article published in 2012, in the *Journal of Marriage and Family*, I read that a warm sibling relationship can be a protective factor during stressful events—parents divorcing, a death in the family.[10] I also read that a warm relationship doesn't have to mean the complete absence of conflict, and that fighting isn't exclusively bad: those who argue learn to deal with difficult emotions, such as jealousy and rage, and, with a bit of luck, acquire some diplomatic skills in the process.[11]

No big surprises there—but of course, all that is precisely my hope for my own children. That they will offer each other friendship, love, and protection, forming a bond that stays with them throughout their lives, as well as the opportunity to become acquainted with disappointment and frustration, with not always getting what they want, with being hurt and feeling remorse.

Because that, the US developmental psychologist Laurie Kramer of the University of Illinois[12] tells me over the phone, is the number one advantage of siblings: while they're little, if the age gap isn't too big and the family is more or less intact, they're there all the time.

"You can scream your head off at them, and the next day they'll still be sitting next to you at the breakfast table," she says.

It means you can't just chase them away by being unbearable. And that sooner or later you'll find the motivation to look for a peaceful resolution.

My tour of the fruits of sibling science has also taught me something else. Namely that Leo Tolstoy's famed observation—that all happy families are alike, while unhappy families are unhappy in their own unique way—is only half true. When it comes to all the damaging and destructive ways in which siblings can influence one another, researchers find patterns as well.

I come across a meta-analysis from 2013, in which the Dutch developmental psychologist Kirsten Buist of Utrecht University examined all the existing research into sibling relationships and psychological and behavioral problems among children and adolescents. Her conclusion: where a warm sibling relationship is generally linked with all sorts of positive outcomes for the brothers and sisters in question, a relationship with a great deal of conflict is often accompanied by depression, loneliness, or aggressive behavior.[13]

The connection she found isn't necessarily a causal one, of course. It's perfectly conceivable that a bad relationship with a sibling makes you lonely or depressed, but it's equally conceivable that a lonely or aggressive child, or a depressed adolescent, is incapable of maintaining a warm bond with a brother or sister.

When I ask about it, one gray morning in a brightly lit conference room at her university, Buist speculates that it probably works both ways, that the two processes reinforce each other.

It makes sense, but it also makes me sad—the image of a lonely child who, due to the armor that loneliness creates, becomes ever more distant from a sibling, only to become lonelier still from the chill that arises between them.

In her meta-analysis, Buist also found that the negative effect of a high-conflict sibling relationship is greater than the positive effect of a warm relationship.

In other words, bad is stronger than good.

For a while, around my son's first birthday, the pile of sibling science articles on my shelf seems to be growing faster than my children. As the relationship between my daughter and son becomes richer and more complex and their shared past gradually makes for a firmer foundation, I read about the relationship between other children, of other parents, in other houses than ours.

Why? For sure, my relentless reading is fueled by a desire for confirmation—confirmation that we've done the right thing, my partner and I, by having a second child. I may also be searching for a new, more merciful light in which to regard my childhood fights with my sister.

But I only partially find what I'm looking for—I learn along the way that only children are not necessarily disadvantaged compared with those who have siblings; that a sibling relationship can work out fairly negatively; that a mean elder sister can do a considerable amount of damage.

It seems like you have a fifty-fifty chance, when you have a second child, of things working out for the better. Apparently, most of us have enough confidence in a good outcome, or we're wary enough of the alternative—an only child—to take the risk.

Or perhaps it's a matter of perspective; perhaps the risk becomes smaller and smaller if you take the long view. In a 2016 book, *Adult Sibling Relationships*, two US psychologists look into what happens to siblings when their childhood days are over. The majority of their survey respondents report being happy with one another's existence, support, and company.[14] The same goes for those who fought a great deal as children (though this study didn't inquire as to whether the fights caused depression, aggression, or loneliness).

The explanation is simple: children become adults. Our world expands, and we learn to put things in perspective and let go of our grievances; we grow up.

Things change—or in any case, our view of things changes.

○

I myself had long forgotten about that cup, the doll's stroller, and the museum. I doubt I would ever have thought of them again if my sister hadn't brought them up. Her memories of our childhood differ from mine, which leads me to suspect that our relationship at the time meant something different to each of us: that what was big for her, for me was too small to remember. What

I saw as unimportant made a lasting impression on her—and vice versa, presumably.

Between my own children I observe an imbalance as well, albeit so far less cruel and heartbreaking. The admiration with which my son looks at my daughter is answered, on her part, with either tenderness or indifference. He imitates her; she encourages him to. He wants to wear her princess dresses; she gives him her least pretty, most worn-out specimen.

It suggests that the way in which siblings influence each other's development works out differently for the first child than for the second. That what we give the first when they gain a brother or sister is not the same as what we give the second—because they are each offered different roles, and a different counterpart.

This is precisely what the Dutch developmental psychologist Sheila van Berkel noticed when, for her PhD thesis, she followed 372 families with two children over the course of four years. She saw that second-borns shared more, listened better, and, according to their parents, were more empathetic than their elder siblings.[15]

Van Berkel offers several possible explanations for these differences: the younger learns from the elder and therefore develops faster in some respects; the younger sees how the elder is treated by their parents and draws lessons from that; and the younger simply has to share more from the outset.

In her study, second-borns also exhibited rebellious

and aggressive behavior somewhat more frequently than firstborns, probably for the same reasons: anyone with an elder sibling has had more experience with conflict and rivalry from an early age, and with observing and imitating childlike aggression.

In order to know whether the differences in behavior persist when children grow up, or venture outside the walls of the parental home, of course you'd have to follow such families far longer and more extensively than was the case in this study.

Other researchers have found that those with an elder sibling who smoked, drank, engaged in criminal activity, or became pregnant in their teens had a substantial chance of following in their footsteps.[16]

There are several possible explanations for such findings. Siblings have a fair share of their genetic material in common, and they usually grow up alongside each other as well. That means they are susceptible to the same outside influences—to a parent or relative setting an example for both, say, or a peer group leaning this way or that. Even so, it seems as if here, too, elder brothers and sisters may serve as an example for those who come after them.

Another possibility is that the first child's behavior creates expectations of how the second will turn out— and that the second child picks up on those expectations, internalizes them, and behaves accordingly.

The relationship between the first and the second is reciprocal but not equal. Because where the second is handed a role model, someone to plot out routes, the first acquires someone to teach and care for. That results in a completely different skill set.

Developmental psychologists have found, for example, that children who make the effort to teach a younger sibling perform better in school than only children or elder children who remain more aloof.[17] Again, the connection may not necessarily be a causal one, but it's not hard to imagine that helping someone younger than ourselves requires us to transpose our own knowledge to a level that the other can understand. That might give our own intelligence a boost as well.

The difference in knowledge and skills can also have less desirable results. For instance, I read about a 2017 experiment conducted by two developmental psychologists from Canada, in which children with siblings turned out more likely to cheat than only children. The larger the age difference, the more likely the elder siblings were to lie about their cheating behavior; and those with a younger sibling also maintained their lie longer than those with an older sibling.[18]

This cup's had a spider in it. That doll's stroller is mine. You have to pay to visit this museum.

My sister and I hardly ever fight anymore. But even now, I'm less magnanimous, less openhearted toward her than I'd like to be, and I share less with her than she might like. I tend to be much better at sharing outside the context of our relationship; I can even be fairly generous. But it's as if we each took on our roles as children and have never been able to shake them off completely—including the associated differences in how we affect each other.

We're not the only ones. After early childhood, too, when an age gap of a couple of years no longer automatically means a substantial difference in power, insight, and manipulative capabilities, the relationship between elder and younger siblings frequently remains imbalanced.

A US study of families with two children in adolescence, for example, examined what happened to these children when they had the impression that their parents favored either themselves or their sibling. It turned out that if the second child thought the first was the favorite, they were much more bothered by it than the first if the first thought the second was the favorite.[19] The reason, the psychologists who conducted the study speculate, is that second-borns compare themselves with their elder siblings more than the other way around.

In a 2017 study, four Dutch researchers found that anyone with a sibling who gets divorced has a greater chance of their own marriage ending in divorce as well; and above all, the effect is stronger for those with an *elder* divorced sibling than for those with a younger divorced sibling.[20]

For a 2006 book, a group of British psychologists interviewed dozens of children to find out how they saw their relationships with their siblings. All interviewees mentioned fights and conflict, but there was a difference between the way elder and younger siblings characterized those conflicts.

Almost without exception, elder children described

their younger brothers and sisters as "irritating" or "annoying." Younger siblings rarely used those words; they ascribed fights to inequality, and to the fact that the elder child was physically or psychologically dominant.[21]

My mother tells me of a picture I once drew in the consulting room of a child psychologist. I was a preschooler at the time and refused to go to sleep at night; at the end of their tether, my parents had called in expert help. The doctor asked me to draw a picture of our family, and apparently I drew my mother as a rabbit, my father as a snake, my sister as a tiny mouse, and myself as a very big horse.

"I looked up to you," my sister says now. "You saw me as a fly, irritatingly buzzing around your ear."

She says it calmly.

I don't have the heart to tell her that, on this front at least, her perception is very much in line with mine.

5

A pack, a tribe, a tornado
Scenes from a family of four

I stop breastfeeding when my son is nine months old. I've kept going for longer this time, in compensation, I suppose, for the lack of undivided attention.

I shove my pump and associated equipment into a corner of the storage cabinet—my partner suggests giving it away or selling it on, but I'm not quite ready for such a resolute end of an era. (Nor for the idea that this second time really is the last.)

A couple of weeks later, I leave for New York. My partner, son, and daughter are staying home together, so the journey is a privilege in several respects. On the plane I order a tomato juice and read *Solitude* by the Canadian author Michael Harris. Harris argues that we need to regain the art of being alone. Creative ideas and existential insights, he writes, emerge best when you spend plenty of time without company.[1]

I suspect Mr. Harris doesn't have children, what with his call for roaming the streets aimlessly for hours on end and his advice that on waking in the morning you first remain supine with your eyes closed for half an hour, rather than immediately springing into action. But I can take it, because the next week is all mine.

I stay at an apartment in my old university neighborhood. The Hudson rushes in the background, and at my feet lie streets and avenues to take me in any direction I please. It's June, not too hot, and my old friends are still around before summer break.

Light as a feather I move through the city, from north to south, across the bridge and back again. The streets smell of musty subway vents and festering trash, a smell I recognize from a time when being alone was not a luxury but a daily reality, a time before I bore responsibility for two small persons.

During the day I hang around in bookshops without buying anything; at the museum I take all the time I want. Over meals out and in conversations in bars I'm wittier than I've been in months; one evening I end up at an impromptu dance party on the East River. Anything is possible, because no one's waiting for me to return.

My partner sends messages from the home front: things are going well there, a touch of sleep deprivation but that's OK, the little ones are good company, it's pleasant weather in the Netherlands too. He sends a photo from the bathroom. My son and daughter are sitting crammed together in the baby bath that we still haven't got rid of: they just fit. The bath is on the tiled floor, my daughter sitting up straight, my son slumped back. He's clutching a rubber duck in each hand.

Do I miss them, the friend I show the photo wants to know. No, I reply, they're having a great time, and actually—I gesture around me—it's *this* I've missed.

On the penultimate day, the weather turns, from sunny and promising to damp and chilly. I take the subway to the park, where a friend of a friend is celebrating his birthday: colorful picnic blankets under a tree, grapes and cheddar cubes and homemade scones on a board, friendly people with interesting lives. One works for the United Nations, another is almost finished with her PhD at Harvard, the next tells me about his PhD in architectural history, and yet another talks about her recent move back to New York, for a job at a gallery.

The responsibilities they bear are big enough—for their bosses, for science, for art. Still, to me, they seem unfettered, these peers of mine who within a year can move to another city and back again, who can work or party until deep in the night because, for them, the morning is flexible.

A drizzle sets in. We shuffle closer together to stay dry under the leafy canopy. I'm underdressed, in my sandals and my short, thin cotton summer dress. Goose pimples creep up my legs. I begin to shiver and feel my shoulders tense up.

We talk about summer plans, about the new president, about cycle paths and brunch restaurants and amazing exhibitions. About real estate, gluten, and ambitions.

No one talks about children, because no one here has any.

And now, I think, now I want to go home.

○

At home, two mornings later, I find at the breakfast table my son in his high chair, my daughter in front of a bowl of "golden yogurt" (flavored with honey), my partner trying to read the newspaper amid their crumbs and cackling. It's the porridge in the grooves of the table, the scent of sleep on the crown of my son's head, the eagerness with which my daughter opens her present— pajamas with all the Disney princesses on them, an immediate hit. It's my partner's breath on my ear, my hand in his hair.

There was a period, before the children, before the *desire* for children, when I couldn't understand why people would ever want it, this whole parenthood thing. Why would you do that, with the person you love most of all? Why would you want to create a new person— whom you might then come to love even more than each other?

I think I hadn't understood then that love isn't a finite resource.

What I also couldn't have known: how magical it is, now and then, to see my partner's gaze in my daughter's eyes. Or to recognize his build, his bone structure, in that of my son.

I also hadn't understood how it would feel to be part of a family, a constellation that feels simultaneously limiting and enriching, that brings us to a halt but also, occasionally, gives us wings.

"The number four has become a pleasant number since the family came to consist of four members," writes the Dutch author Anna Enquist in her novel *Contrapunt* (*Counterpoint*). "The points of the compass and the seasons, rather than the Three Kings and the Trinity, the mother thinks. She can hoist a child onto each hip and run away, if necessary. The family has precisely the right proportions: four chairs at the table, four seats in the car, two by two on their bikes."[2]

○

At first there were two of us, then two adults with a baby. Now that our family consists of four members, the dynamic has changed again. Our specific gravity has increased; my partner and I no longer form a majority. We're adapting to this new reality, the reality of the standard family.

As a family of four, we move slowly and our radius of activity is limited. Entire Saturday mornings are consumed with getting dressed, waiting for one to wake up, going back to bed with the other, halfheartedly forging plans.

Now and again we're more resolute. One day we head for the dunes. It's colder than expected, the wind piercing; my daughter's coat isn't thick enough, and my son refuses to stay in the stroller but doesn't want to be carried either.

He bellows, my daughter cries, our fingers are freezing, and five hundred meters in we turn around, head back to the car, back home.

○

Sometimes I attempt, very early in the morning, to start the day ahead of the troops. In the dark I pull on my sports clothes and tiptoe in my socks to the front door, where I've strategically positioned my running shoes the night before.

But our apartment isn't built for a family, all the rooms are open to each other, and nine times out of ten I give myself away with a creaking stair, the sound of the key in the lock. Then there's a cry from my son, a "Mummy!" from my daughter, or a sighed supplication from my sleepy partner that causes me to turn around and return, defeated, to the nest.

Sometimes my partner and I try to have a conversation over dinner: we're constantly interrupted, often unable even to hear each other. Or we manage, but it's all about logistics—who's dropping off and picking up tomorrow, who'll do the shopping at the weekend, and what to do about the babysitter who's canceled.

After the meal: the predictable mantra of bath and bed, undoing the destruction, and then early to bed ourselves.

Under the covers, I find him, tell him I miss him.

○

"I saw you on your bike," an acquaintance messages me. "You're a force to be reckoned with!"

Cycling with my children—my son in front, my daughter in the seat behind me, I'm a kind of Mother Goose, upright and resolute.

When I push them forth in the double stroller, my shoulders hunched and my back slightly bowed, I'm a beast of burden.

○

We go on a bike ride, each with a child onboard, stop for lunch at a café in a nearby village. While my partner settles the bill, the three of us head over to the playground on the other side of the road, my daughter in front of me, my son behind.

Between the road and the playground is a ditch. There's duckweed on the surface, and my son, who doesn't yet know what that means, steps onto it, and then immediately straight through. In a second I've jumped in beside him, and I'm standing up to my waist in the water and see him sinking, facedown and motionless, his light green jacket bulging briefly before disappearing under the dark green covering.

I pull him out.

He cries, but no louder than usual: the warm shower, a bit later, at the house of friends who happen to have moved to the village, bothers him more.

My daughter is more severely shocked. "I don't want my little brother to drown," she says when we cycle home, my son in a dress lent to us by our friends, me in borrowed tracksuit bottoms.

That night I sleep badly, suddenly conscious of the vulnerability of our foursome, the fragility, the difference a couple of seconds can make.

What if, I mumble to my partner, what if I'd been looking at my phone just at that moment? What if I hadn't seen where he went down? What if?

"But you did see," he replies, "and it all worked out fine."

○

One Sunday afternoon at the end of autumn, we're invited to drinks by a couple we don't know very well. We enter their elegant house, an unraveling bundle of winter coats, boots, bags, diapers. I blow out the carefully placed candles on the coffee table, to be on the safe side.

We drink wine, have a more or less coherent conversation about the changing neighborhood, changing career plans. The cheese that appears on the table is almost instantly devoured by our children; a half-full glass of water tips over, its contents spilling across the floor. My daughter discovers the piano, and my son pulls the tail of the tiny young kitten our hostess brought home earlier that day.

When we leave, not much later, I have the feeling we're leaving a scene of devastation behind, and yet I'm not ashamed. That's who we are now, I think: a pack, a tribe, a tornado.

And it's exactly as it should be.

6

Thou shalt not compare

How we measure our children
against each other

Our first child was our only child. She came without material for comparison. We knew other people with babies and children, but we didn't see them often enough to base very specific expectations on them.

We also didn't really care, I think. "People without children," Rachel Cusk observes in *A Life's Work*, "don't seem very interested in anything that people with have to say about it: they approach parenthood blithely, as if they were the first, with all the innocence of Adam and Eve before the fall."[1]

Our daughter was our first and only child, and she taught us who she was. Sui generis, on her own terms. Of course, there were the pediatrician graphs, against which her own development was measured once in a while, but those were abstract, generalized gauges with little influence on how we saw our daughter. (Had she been ill, or colicky, or her development disrupted, it would undoubtedly have been a different story—but, as it was, we were able to be every bit as blithe as the parents of Cusk's description.)

With our second child, things were different. We knew, more or less, what we were starting out on. The comparisons commenced as soon as I was pregnant. In contrast to our first, our second didn't arrive precisely on his due date. "He's late," I grumbled when I woke up that morning, my belly as big and round as it had been the night before.

At his birth, less than twenty-four hours later, he was heavier than his sister.

After the birth, he cried longer and louder and more heartrendingly than she had.

He fed more and more frequently.

Her expression, in those early weeks, often had a fierce quality to it, somewhat furious, even; he looked more shocked and worried (I thought).

After eight weeks, she slept for twelve hours at night; his sleep pattern remained erratic and unpredictable for more than a year.

He walked a month later, his tantrums didn't last as long, and where her first word had been "apple," his was "that."

○

Our daughter turns four and starts school. The first Monday morning of the new year we drop her off, my partner, my son, and I. It's still dark outside and ice-cold. Electric light tumbles through the school's windowpanes and is reflected by the still-damp paving stones. The effect is cinematic.

The scene in the school playground feels simultaneously familiar and surreal. I remember precisely how it felt to walk into a noisy, jittery stream of children like that, on their way to an entrance, to the start of the day.

But never before had I done it as a parent, and never before had I realized that this is a daily ritual for adults too. It's only the first time, but I can already discern the contours of a new routine.

My daughter is quiet, stoical, and curious. The teacher offers her hand, and she answers the gesture with an embrace. She's invited onto the teacher's lap.

My son waves, his eyes wide.

From that day, for the first time since my maternity leave, my son and I spend a morning a week together, just the two of us. With his sister at school, my attention is undivided.

We begin the days slowly, in and around the kitchen table. I tidy things up; he takes them out again. We take our time with getting dressed, and with what comes afterward. What we do doesn't much matter—as long as we're at the school gate at half past twelve.

It reminds me of the period before he was here, when my daughter was his age and I would take her to the library on weekday mornings, or to the zoo, or for coffee with other mothers and fathers with small children.

Back then I'd found it exhausting, all those hours out and about with a child. Now it's easy: compared with the days when I have both of them with me, the time with one child is uncluttered and peaceful, calm and cozy.

He's changing, I notice on such mornings. Or perhaps it's my image of him that's changing—that's possible too. He understands more, wants more, and is capable of more than before, or more than I realized until now.

The changes are subtle. That he knows what I mean when I say we're going to the shop, points out where my shoes are when I've misplaced them, knows the meaning of words he can't yet pronounce but has clearly stored.

I hadn't previously noticed that he'd come so far, that he could already do all this.

Perhaps it's because normally my daughter's a bit quicker off the mark with looking for the shopping bag, finding my shoes, naming the world around us.

Or, perhaps, it's because all that time I've been preoccupied with keeping an eye on two children, focusing mainly on their mutual bond and interactions—and maybe that's made it harder to follow their individual development.

In any case, only now that his big sister's not standing next to him do I get an idea of how much he's grown up.

○

One Wednesday morning, not long after the conversation in which my sister confronted me with the bully I once was, I cycle to a conference room with a suspended ceiling on the edge of town. There, along with ten other parents, I'm to take part in a parenting course on sibling rivalry.

Parenting courses, like parenting books, are a modern phenomenon—a sign, perhaps, that the "correct" way of raising children concerns us more than ever. And, in particular, that we believe that the correct way exists in the first place.

I've joined this course because I'm curious as to how that hunger for advice is catered to—by the market, by experts. But my presence is also, in part, a form of penance: my sister's stories have made me feel guilty in retrospect, and I somehow hope to atone for my childhood sins through my own children.

The sibling scientist and developmental psychologist Laurie Kramer, who has worked on the subject for years, once told me about a study she conducted with a colleague. They had asked more than fifty mothers of two children how they looked back on their own childhood in general, and on their relationship with their siblings in particular. They also interviewed the mothers on the behavior of their own children: how they interacted, how close their relationship was, how often they fought or were kind to each other. Finally, they observed the children playing together.

It turned out that the children of mothers who remembered growing up with a sibling as complicated or painful often behaved more positively toward each other than those of mothers who characterized their relationship with their sibling as pleasant and relatively problem-free. They played together more, helped each other more often, shared more jokes, and worked harder to resolve disagreements. It was as if mothers from the latter category automatically assumed that things would work out fine for their own offspring, so they didn't particularly work at making that expectation a reality.

Mothers less fortunate in their sibling relationships tried to foster a good relationship between their children as much as possible and to avoid their parents' mistakes, as far as they were able to identify them. When their children fought, for example, they helped them end the fight by looking for a resolution that was more or less satisfactory to both parties.[2]

This study, small as it was, suggests that while new generations build on the work of preceding generations, they partially undo that work as well. Our parents protect us from certain sidesteps, and as a result, it doesn't even occur to us to do the same for our own children.

Upbringing isn't just something that happens between parents and children: the preceding and following generations participate as well.

The cheerful, friendly instructor asks us to form groups of two and describe our children to each other. I'm paired with a mother who, during the round of introductions, told us about the constant fighting between her two daughters, coming close to tears as she recounted it.

She'd smiled bravely, and I'd thought of my own parents. I too had occasionally found my mother crying on the edge of the bed, her hands over her ears, after my sister and I had fought yet again over more bathroom time or a particular top with an asymmetrical neckline.

I start with our eldest. I describe her as sensitive, clever, and curious, and somewhat afraid of failure. She's sharp and funny and easily upset. The youngest, I say, is more emotionally stable and perhaps also rather more cheerful. Physically he's less clumsy, more adventurous. Socially, good-humored and kind, but also quicker to anger.

And there I go again, I think. I'm making comparisons.

It's not even that the comparison is to the advantage or disadvantage of the first or second child. Nor am I disappointed that he doesn't "live up to" the standard my daughter has set—or, vice versa, that he in some sense does "better" than she does.

It's the very *existence* of a standard, a norm. That when I look at one, I immediately see similarities and differences to the other. That I describe my son with my daughter in mind—and that I do so constantly. Because she's effectively always ahead of him, enjoys a head start of more than two and a half years.

Call me romantic, but it strikes me as fairer for a child to go through life without a yardstick. To be seen as they *are*, not in contrast to someone else. At the same time, I don't know how else to do it: human beings have a deep-rooted tendency to make comparisons. It happens automatically.

The mother of two with whom I'm partnered listens patiently and watches me with gentle, sympathetic eyes. She smiles and nods and asks if it's her turn.

Her eldest daughter, she says, is curious and very imaginative. Her youngest is levelheaded, down-to-earth, mischievous. You can have a great laugh with her, says the mother.

Oh, I think, as I listen to the way she describes her children—separately, without comparing them—so it's possible after all.

Parents who openly compare their children, the instructor explains later that day, may inadvertently create the conditions for rivalry, or at least contribute to them.

She confirms what I fear on my anxious days: that my tendency to describe one child with the other in mind will also be expressed in my behavior, in ways I'm perhaps only barely aware of myself. That my son's enthusiasm, for instance, will make me cheerful in part due to the contrast with my daughter's morning moodiness—or the other way around. That it'll make me that much nicer to the one who makes me feel happy. And that all those subconscious signals together will shape my children, give them the feeling that I don't just love them as they are, bring them to see each other as competitors.

Of course, there are plenty of other conceivable causes

of sibling rivalry, I think as the instructor continues talking. Developmental psychologist Laurie Kramer, the one who studied how a mother's own childhood experiences trickled down to the way she raised her children, told me that it had long been believed, in her field, that children fought to gain their parents' attention. But when researchers observed and interviewed siblings, they came to very different conclusions: most fights, she told me, arose because one had irritated the other, or because one had something the other wanted. Parents could play a role in the continuation of such fights, but often enough, they had nothing whatsoever to do with their taking place to begin with.

There's a good chance I'm overestimating my influence on my children.[3] And perhaps I'm also underestimating my own capacity to compensate for all those subconscious tendencies, all those failings big and small that are probably unavoidable anyway. Because even if humans are inclined to make comparisons, that doesn't mean you have to behave accordingly.

The remedy put forward by the instructor is as simple as it is fundamental, and comes, workshop style, in the form of concrete examples:

> Don't tell the youngest he should eat nicely like his elder sister, just say you can see he's playing with his food.
>
> Don't say your daughter gets upset so much faster than her little brother, just say you see a girl crying, and ask her to help you understand her tears.

Don't project, don't compare, just look—and describe
what you see, child by child.

When I cycle home at the end of the day, a long ride along
the river into a bracing wind, I hope that soon I will be
asked again to describe my children.

Next time I'll do it differently: I won't describe them
in terms of each other. Because if the way we see our
children influences the way we approach them, then perhaps the opposite is also true: that a different view of your
children can begin quite simply with a different way of
speaking—both with them and about them.

Typical second child

On the myth of the birth-order effect

One Friday afternoon at a party, I'm sitting in a garden next to a young mother of two. Her baby is only a couple of weeks old and is lying on her chest, out for the count. They'd taken a long time, she tells me, to come up with a name for their second child. After all, they'd already used their favorite name: it had gone to their first.

On the scale of a human life, it's small-fry, but as a metaphor I find it significant. I think of the proverbs we have around second times—second choice, second place, second fiddle, eternal second. I think of Buzz Aldrin, always in the shadow of the one who went before him, out there on the moon. I think of my sister and my son: both second children.

Thanks to the findings of sibling scientists, I now know that firstborns and second-borns are shaped by each other, each in their own way. But I continue to wonder whether one of them doesn't end up drawing the short straw.

I was the first child in our family, the eldest, numero uno. I was also fearful of failure, neurotic, a perfectionist, ambitious—undoubtedly to the point of being unbearable. My sister didn't study as hard and went out more, worked at every trendy bar in town and spent many an after-school afternoon horizontal, on the sofa, in front of the TV.

I've long attributed the differences in our characters to the different positions we held in our family. It seemed to me, all things considered, better to be the first: you had to work harder to expand the boundaries your parents set for you, blazed a trail for your generation yourself, had a greater sense of responsibility, more persistence, and emerged, in the end, more self-confident.

That theory worked in my favor, but during my pregnancy I started to feel sorry for my son. Through no fault of his own, he'd missed out on the enviable position of firstborn. It took that sense of pity for me to realize that I could try to uncover the basis of my ideas about the personality traits of first and second children—and whether there was anything to them.

What I hadn't expected was that the trail of my assumptions would lead to one of the most controversial subjects in the social sciences.

O

It was 1874, and Francis Galton, an intellectual all-rounder and a half cousin of Charles Darwin, published *English Men of Science: Their Nature and Nurture*. These were the early days of psychology: the belief in objective science, in measuring things as the key to knowledge, was enjoying its heyday. Like many other thinkers of that period, Galton was interested in the factors that determined a person's success in life. In his book, he profiled one hundred and eighty prominent scientists, and in the course of his research Galton noticed something peculiar: among his subjects, firstborns were overrepresented.[1]

Galton's observation was the first in a long line of scientific and pseudoscientific publications on the subject: on the effect of your place in the family on the course of your life—on the *birth-order effect*. The greater chance of success for firstborns, in Galton's view, was because of their upbringing, an explanation that fitted in with the mores of the Victorian era: eldest sons had a greater chance of having their education paid for by their parents, parents gave their eldest sons more attention as well as responsibility, and in families of limited financial resources, parents might care just a little bit better for their firstborns. The distribution system at the foundation of this is called primogeniture: the right of the eldest son (or considerably less frequently, the eldest daughter) as heir.[2]

Primogeniture was widespread for a long time in Europe, I learn when I read up on the history of family relationships.

Among Portuguese nobility in the fifteenth and

sixteenth centuries, for example, second- and later-born sons were sent to the front as soldiers more often than firstborn sons. Second and subsequent daughters were more likely than eldest daughters to end up in the convent.[3]

In Venice in the sixteenth and seventeenth centuries, it was generally the eldest brother who was permitted to marry, after which younger brothers would live with him and his family, dependent and subservient.[4]

Primogeniture is also one of the reasons why, in fairy tales, conflict between brothers is often the most fierce.[5] After all, as a British historian once put it, "The manner of splitting property is the manner of splitting people."[6]

Apart from a few royal families, primogeniture is no longer the norm in Western countries. At most it plays a role in family businesses. Somewhere in the course of the last century, most residents of industrialized countries became convinced that all our children had a right to precisely the same—that love, attention, time, and inheritance should be divided equally and fairly.

That's what my partner and I strive to achieve: equal treatment of our two children, no hierarchy at home. But then we can't get around the fact that first, second, and subsequent children all have slightly different starting points. The question is precisely what consequences that has, and how insurmountable they are.

At the beginning of the twentieth century, Alfred Adler, Freud's erstwhile follower, the one who believed that the arrival of a younger sibling meant the dethronement of the firstborn, introduced the birth-order effect into the domain of personality psychology. According to Adler, the eldest identifies most with the adults in his environment and therefore develops both a greater sense of responsibility and more neuroses. The youngest has the greatest chance of being spoiled and is also, often, more creative. All children in the middle—Adler himself was a middle child—are emotionally more stable and independent: they're the peacemakers, the diplomats, used to sharing from the start, and therefore less demanding.[7]

After Galton and Adler, the idea that family position affects personality has been subjected to many a scientific test. These tests generated a series of factoids that undoubtedly still fly across the table at Christmas dinners: that firstborn children are overrepresented as Nobel Prize winners,[8] composers of classical music,[9] and, funnily enough, among "prominent psychologists."[10] Subsequent children, on the other hand, were more likely to have supported the Protestant Reformation and the French Revolution.[11]

A friend, the eldest out of her nest of four, presses into my hands a book that her mother claims to have been all the rage among parents she knew during the 1990s. The title is *Brothers and Sisters: The Order of Birth in the Family,* and it was written in the mid-twentieth century by the Viennese pediatrician and anthroposophist Karl König.

What strikes me from the very first pages is the certainty with which König characterizes first, second, and third children—as if the birth-order effect were a law of nature, whereby A inevitably leads to B. For example, he quotes a study conducted in the early twentieth century stating that a first child is "more likely to be serious, sensitive," "conscientious," and "good" and—this is my favorite—"fond of books."

Later on, these first children can become "shy, even fearful," *or* they become "self-reliant, independent." A second child, by contrast, is "placid, easy-going, friendly [and] cheerful"—unless they are "stubborn, rebellious, independent (or apparently so)" and "able to take a lot of punishment."[12]

These typologies most resemble horoscopes, in the sense that it can't have been difficult, in the 1950s any more than now, to recognize yourself at least partially in any of them. Amenable or stubborn, anxious or self-assured—you've pretty much covered the entire spectrum there.

So I go back online, in search of clarification. By now, studies looking into the birth-order effect number in the thousands, and approaches and methods vary considerably—from case studies of psychiatric patients to qualitative interviews to the analysis of large data sets.

There's no shortage of popular publications either: in recent decades, titles such as *Born to Rebel: Birth Order, Family Dynamics, and Creative Lives* and *Birth Order Blues: How Parents Can Help Their Children Meet the Challenges of Birth Order* have helped spread the idea that your place in the family determines who you are.

In 2003, two US and two Polish psychologists asked hundreds of participants, from university undergraduates and high school students to a representative sample drawn from the Polish population, what they knew about birth order. The majority of respondents were convinced that those born earlier had a greater chance of a prestigious career than those born later, and that those different career opportunities had to do with their specific birth-order-related character traits.

In sum, a century after the possible existence of the birth-order effect was first proposed, it had become common knowledge.[13] That knowledge is now so common, in fact, that it lends itself to satire: "Study Shows Eldest Children Are Intolerable Wankers," a headline on the Dutch satirical news website *De Speld* quipped in early 2018.

Nevertheless, there is plenty of criticism of birth-order theories and the associated empirical research. I don't have to dig for long in the mountain of birth-order studies to come across the caveats.

It's not at all straightforward, critics point out, to know what you're measuring when attempting to unravel the factors that shape an individual human life. And it's very difficult to exclude all the "noise," as physicists in a laboratory would be able to do more easily. There's a substantial chance that traits we might attribute to a person's birth order have more to do with, say, socioeconomic status, the size or ethnicity of the family, or the values of a particular culture.

In order to properly research whether the birth-order effect exists, you'd have to use gigantic data sets. Ideally, you wouldn't just compare first, second, and third children from different families, but also children from the same family, at the same age. That's a daunting task, and few studies satisfy that requirement. (Birth-order effect pioneer Francis Galton drew his generalized conclusions, for example, on the basis of fewer than two hundred "English men of science"—a tiny sample, and not exactly a cross-section of British society.)

It's enough to drive a person crazy, I think: so many assumptions, so much research, so few hard conclusions—although I suppose the latter is often the case, in the social sciences. They tend to provide more nuance rather than painting things in black and white—and rightly so.

But I need to know if there's a counterargument to be made, in response to the certainty with which a friend remarks that second children are always "much more chill" than first children. Or to the way a family member takes it for granted that our son, independent and sociable as he is, is a "typical second child."

Is there a counterargument?

Yes, certainly. In the past few years, considerably more reliable research has become available regarding the personality traits of first and second children. The end of 2015 saw the publication of two studies in which the methodological shortcomings of previous birth-order

research (unrepresentative sample sets, incorrect infer-
ences) were largely obviated.

In one of these studies, two US psychologists analyzed data about the personality traits and family position
of 377,000 secondary school pupils in the United States.
They did find associations between birth order and personality, but besides being tiny—"statistically significant
but meaningless," as one of the researchers formulated
it—they also partially ran counter to those predicted by
the prevailing theories. For instance, firstborn children in
this data set might be a little more cautious, but they were
also less neurotic than later-born children.[14]

The other study looked for the relationship between
personality and birth order in data from the United
States, Britain, and Germany for a total of more than
twenty thousand people. The researchers compared both
children from different families and siblings from the
same family, and corrected for factors such as family size
and age.

This study was more extensive and precise than anything that had gone before. Here, too, the results were
disillusioning, at least for those who believe that eldest
children as a rule are more responsible and youngest
children more rebellious. The researchers in fact found
no relationship between a person's place in the family
and any personality trait whatsoever, be it extroversion,
kindness, emotional stability, diligence, or imagination.[15]

It's a relief, I note, to read their conclusions. As if my

children have been given a little extra room to maneuver, a larger field, free of set routes. Whoever my son is or will become, his character has not, or in any case not only, been determined by the blindly coincidental fact of his having arrived second. My relief is conditional, of course—science, after all, has a tendency to change its mind. But apparently for me, for now, it's sufficient.

And now? The results of these two studies suggest that the birth-order effect on personality does not exist, that it's a fable, the authors write in an accompanying article.

Nevertheless, they cherish little hope of ridding the world of that fable.[16] After all, they write, it takes forever for academic insights to trickle down to the general public. And in any case, we tend to be swayed less by scientific results than by our own personal experiences.

Perhaps what's more important, they write, is that the belief in the existence of the birth-order effect is so stubborn because it's easily confused with age. Pretty much everyone can see with their own eyes that older children (who were born earlier) behave differently from younger children (who were born later). And there's a good chance that a first child, when compared with a second child, will *appear* more cautious and anxious. It's just that this difference probably has more to do with age than with birth order.

The second child is quicker to anger, I had said to that other mother in the parenting course. But hadn't my daughter been just as irascible when she was my son's age?

I'd described him as more emotionally stable. Perhaps what I'd meant is that I can quite easily discern his emotions, which for now are relatively basic. They're still so close to the surface: his entire face joins in when he's angry, or happy, or sad. He sulks when something doesn't go his way, bows his head and looks askance when he's doing something he knows isn't really allowed, throws everything within reach on the floor when he's angry. When he's excited, he wags, even in the absence of a tail. His sister's feelings have already grown more subtle and complex, and the way they're expressed has become hard to read, for her as well as for me.

That difference in age might also be the reason that children from the same family are often assigned specific roles, the psychologist Kirsten Buist tells me when I present her with the two US scientists' hypothesis. Although research suggests there are no fixed differences in personality, we might impose them to some extent. Parents tell the eldest to be responsible, and the youngest to listen to the eldest. The behavior that follows from this is an expression of that role, not of a person's character—but good luck making that distinction with the naked eye.

I think of the way we tried to prepare my daughter for the arrival of her little brother. How, to avoid disappointment, we refrained from telling her there would soon be someone she could play with and instead said that there would be someone who couldn't do anything at all. She'd be able to explain everything to him, we'd said, because she already knew so much, was so very capable.

The prospect had certainly appealed to her.

Little did we know we were talking her into a stereotype-perpetuating role.

○

In the early 1990s, a group of political scientists observed with barely concealed exasperation that birth order had been "linked to a truly staggering range of behaviors."[17] They for their part tried to debunk the myth that even a person's political preferences were determined by their position in the family by reviewing studies that addressed, among other things, whether firstborns had "an uncommon tendency to enter into political careers," were more conservative than those born later, and were more likely to hold political office. Their meta-analysis failed to find consistent patterns—but did find myriad methodological flaws.

The controversy invoked by the subject is fascinating enough, but what fascinates me even more is the longing that seems to fuel the persistence of scientists and laypeople alike. It's a longing to confirm that our children's place in the family ranking has marked them for life.

Of course, *all* the circumstances in which a child comes into the world—whether they're born male or female, in war or peace, into relative poverty or exorbitant wealth—end up making a person who they are. But the birth-order effect seems to particularly enthuse and pre-occupy us.

Perhaps because it's so concrete: it's rather more fun and more satisfying to attribute a small baby's generous smile to the fact that he's a second child than to a vague interplay of personality and environment, expectations and discernment.

Such concreteness and simplicity are especially attractive, I suppose, if we attribute the effect to ourselves. It absolves us for a moment of the responsibility for who we are and the duty to make ourselves what we want to become: my neuroticism isn't my fault, it's just because I'm the eldest.

My son began to dole out little smiles when he was barely four weeks old. They were not just twitches or reflexes, I knew for sure, but outright attempts at contact. He began smiling earlier than his sister had, and this made sense to me: he was the second child, after all, and so the more sociable one, just like my own sister.

It didn't occur to me in that moment that this interpretation of mine was founded on stories we'd been passing on for generations, packaged in throwaway remarks like "typical second child" or "because I'm the eldest . . ."

It's only now that I'm beginning to understand that those stories have a history. And that, without us really realizing it, they might shape our children's present as well as their future.

Shall we read a story together?

What parents do differently the second time around

My son points to a bright green stuffed toy frog with a red scarf around its neck, rummaged out of his sister's basket. For a couple of months he's been dragging the toy everywhere. Frog has to come on the bike, to daycare, to the sandpit, and to bed. My son sucks on Frog's hand as I kiss him good night.

Every night it occurs to me that I really ought to wash the creature, which looks increasingly revolting and is probably harboring more and more germs each day.

Every morning I forget.

Second children have a reduced chance of asthma, eczema, and allergies compared with first children. Second-borns aren't exempt from these ailments, but it's less common for them to have them.[1]

I read this in an article in *Allergy: European Journal of Allergy and Clinical Immunology*. It's not daily reading for me, but I still haven't finished with the birth-order effect, or the birth-order effect hasn't finished with me.

And although I'm alert to the fables going around about the influence of one's place in the family, I find this easy to believe. When it comes to asthma, eczema, and allergies, I have the full package; my sister's lungs, on the other hand, function perfectly—and her skin is flawless.

So that's how it works, with averages and probabilities and general claims based on lots of data: it's so much easier to assume they're true when you recognize yourself in them.

So much easier to believe that sibling rivalry is inevitable when you see your own children fighting.

So much easier to believe global warming is real when you encounter one heat wave after another. Or that such a thing as pregnancy discrimination exists when a friend, while expecting her second, is told in a job interview that she shouldn't really want it anyway, this challenging job that demands she perform to the best of her abilities.

To make sure, I call a pediatrician who specializes in lung diseases and allergies. It's true, he says, and the most cited explanation comes from the hygiene hypothesis. Those with elder siblings are exposed to a lot more germs at a young age than firstborns—there's no one as filthy as a toddler, after all. That gives the immune system a better chance to develop, making it less inclined to overreact to stimuli that can't really do any harm.

The rising number of people with asthma, eczema, and allergies in industrialized countries is therefore in part related to shrinking family size. There are fewer children with at least one elder sibling, so there are more children with a higher chance of contracting these conditions.

Of course, the fact that households in general have become rather cleaner plays a role as well. In some ways, hygiene makes us less resilient. My mother tells me she changed my bedding twice a day when I was a newborn, and vacuumed at least as often. Now that I have a second child myself, I'm pretty sure she gave up on that regime when my sister came along. And this, this change in parental behavior when a second child enters the mix, suggests that it's *parents* who are, ultimately, responsible for the existence of many a birth-order effect.

○

The idea that birth order has a predictable effect on your personality—on how well behaved or ambitious you are, how willful or introverted—is in all likelihood no more than that, an idea. But that doesn't mean we have to throw the entire birth-order effect out with the bathwater.

A group of academics who are interested in the effect of birth order on physical and cognitive outcomes *do* find effects. And those effects say a lot, not only about first and second children, but also about their parents.

Besides a connection between birth order and asthma and eczema, for instance, there is also a link with diabetes: firstborn children are at a higher risk. The same goes for high blood pressure—although epidemiologists are still groping in the dark as to how that comes to be the case.[2]

Birth order also seems to have an effect on height. The more children in a family, the shorter they are on average; and the second is affected more by this than the first, and the third and fourth even more again.[3] (And height is often used as a gauge of health.) Scientists have put forward several possible reasons for why this might be so. For one thing, studies have found that children with elder siblings are less likely to receive all their vaccinations, and parents are less inclined to call in expert help when their younger children are ill. Children with elder siblings also eat junk food more frequently at a young age. And the more children a woman already has, the smaller her chance of following a healthy diet during pregnancy.[4]

I remember the wedding of my sister-in-law, in the baking-hot central region of France. My daughter was one and a half, my son not yet on the way, and the family stuck around for the day after the festivities.

That evening my nephews and nieces were all given an ice cream. Did our daughter want one as well, we were asked. No, we said, she'd never had ice cream, and she was only one and a half, so why would she?

Three years later, when the four of us went to the ice-cream parlor for the first ice cream of spring, it didn't even occur to us that our son, aged one and a half, could miss out.

The rules you draw up for raising a first child, the habits you develop, won't always withstand the extra pressure a second child brings.

That said, the second child is certainly not always the one to draw the short straw—the reduced risk of asthma and related misery are a case in point. In addition, I come across a long-running study among a cross-section of the British population, suggesting that children with an elder sibling suffer less frequently from psychological problems than eldest children.[5]

It may be that elder brothers or sisters serve as a kind of buffer in times of social stress. Another possible explanation, according to one of the researchers, is that a second child, more often than a first, is born into a family that is already "prepared for family life"—more stable, perhaps, and hence better able to offer a secure, dependable environment for a child to grow up in.[6]

"We already had everything in place," says a mother I know, with some satisfaction, when she talks about the birth, a few months earlier, of her second daughter. "All those extra-soft towels and absorbent diapers and milk bottles and hot water bottles and the sling and the stroller. We didn't have to rush around worrying about all that this time."

She looks relaxed, much more so than a couple of years ago, when her eldest daughter had just been born. I suspect that the things she lists are a metaphor for a less tangible form of "everything in place"—that what she really means is that she and her partner were over the first shock of parenthood when the second one arrived, that they'd already adopted a way of life that could relatively easily make way for a new, small, dependent element.

Something like that, I think, is what my own mother means when she says that the second child is much less of "an experiment" than the first: that the first child gives his or her parents practice, and that practice pays off.

The open-mindedness with which my partner and I welcomed our daughter was always something I saw as an advantage—far more romantic to be the first and only, terra incognita, than a variation on a theme your parents already know. But perhaps it's not so bad, appearing onstage after it's already been set.

On my computer, I keep a list of more and less certain birth-order effects.

Personality: no effect.

Height: the first child has better prospects.

Chance of asthma, high blood pressure, and diabetes: the second child has a lower risk.

Chance of psychological problems in times of stress: on average, the second child is better placed.

It's as if I'm hoping for a final score, a judgment. As if I'm fishing for a conclusion—that it's on balance better to be the first child, or the second. Or better still, that the pros and cons cancel one another out, so that first and second children come off equally well.

It's a ridiculous exercise, of course—if only because the next study might negate or add nuance to some of these findings, if only because in the end, those average heights and risks of allergies say very little about the two specific individuals for whom I'm totting up the score. My daughter doesn't have asthma, my son does have eczema, so there you go already.

Yet I continue to search, continue to add to my list. And I think it's because deep down I still fear that the fact that there are two of them will turn out, one way or another, to be "unfair." That one of the two, by complete coincidence, will get a "better deal," a better starting position—and that it's best to be aware of this as a parent, so you can compensate for it.

But of course a quest like that is too cold, too calculating.

As if the way in which a family constellation turns out for one child can be set against the way it turns out for the other. As if we could bring in an accountant to constantly watch and note down all our choices and impulses, all our mistakes and strokes of luck, in a life-size Excel spreadsheet. So that in the end, underneath the bottom line, we could have two exactly equivalent results appear. As if people aren't erratic, the world not full of surprises.

Apparently, I'm inclined to see my children as the potential winners and losers of our family, ironically enough in a competition in which most of the cards have already been dealt.

Apparently, I somehow believe that one child's gain automatically comes at the cost of the other, as if there's a limited quantity of happiness and success available to the two of them, a common pool from which they must both draw. (It's a legacy, perhaps, of the way I've long thought about love: that it was finite, and that the love you felt for your child would be subtracted from the love you felt for the father of that child.)

Whereas, in fact, our coexistence as a family of four feels more like a complex choreography than a competition. Our pack practices at routine, not for a race. Winner takes all, survival of the fittest: it's an absurd lens through which to view family life.

And yet, that seems to be just the kind of lens used by the latest group of researchers to immerse themselves in the birth-order effect: economists. For the past fifteen years or so, they too have been examining the ways in which our position in the family affects us. They're specifically interested in the sort of clear, measurable issues that preoccupied Francis Galton a century and a half ago: IQ, cognitive skills, and school performance. The sorts of issues, in short, that determine a person's "human capital."

In their studies, these economists not only compare children from different families with one another, but also look at siblings within the same family. In doing so, they make use of unprecedentedly large databases. These databases, collected and maintained by census bureaus and other institutions, including the military, contain detailed information on entire populations, from Norway and Sweden to the state of California.

And here it comes: based on this data, economists find consistent birth-order effects.[7] The most noteworthy: as in Galton's *English Men of Science*, firstborn children generally have the best chance of "success."

For instance, a 2007 study in which a group of US economists scrutinized data from the entire male population of Norway, found that, on average, first-borns' IQ scores were three points higher than those of second-borns.[8] A study from 2016, among a large group of Americans, noted that second children had a 3 percent lower probability of finishing high school, and on average received half a year less education than first children.[9]

Other studies, carried out in different countries, found similar effects.[10] "It now seems clear," two economists wrote in 2016 in the *Journal of Human Resources*, "that for those born and raised in high-income countries . . . earlier-born children enjoy higher wages and education as adults."[11]

The fact that this applies to high-income countries— such as Norway, the United States, or the Netherlands, for example—is significant. Economists who investigated the link between birth order and human capital in Ecuador, the Philippines, and Ethiopia discovered the opposite effect: there, the eldest often enjoyed less education.

The explanation: in poor countries with less of a social safety net, it's often the firstborn who is taken out of school to contribute to the family income. Younger siblings can continue to attend, thanks in part to the efforts of the eldest.[12]

To be sure, three IQ points is a meaningless difference—you would never know it from speaking to someone, the developmental psychologist Sheila van Berkel explains to me. In fact, you wouldn't notice anything anywhere, except on an IQ test.

Since the effects found in these studies are about averages, they also say little about what it means, for any random individual, to be the second child. It says little about my son or my sister. And although school achievements and IQ have the advantage of being measurable, they only measure a person's specific skills in that one specific moment in time.

All the same, there is an effect.

Moreover, a study of the relationship between IQ and birth order in Norwegian men concluded that this effect disappeared for second children whose elder brother or sister had died at a young age.

Those second children became "de facto" first children—and scored accordingly.[13] That means the effect probably has nothing to do with biological differences between first and second children, that it's not *nature* causing the effect but differences in the way they're treated—in *nurture*.

In other words, it looks like many parents behave differently toward their first and second children. And this has consequences, however small, for the cognitive development of those children.

The explanations scientists put forward for this unequal treatment are quite banal, and formulated as though they belong in an annual report, rather than the annals of family life.

According to the *confluence hypothesis*, when it comes to the first couple of years of life, a first child spends most of their time with their parents, while a second child also has to contend with a sibling from the outset. And since the average toddler is rather less "cognitively stimulating" than an adult, the second child's development lags behind in that respect.

Elder children may also benefit from educating and supervising their younger siblings by reinforcing for themselves what they're teaching, while their younger siblings, as a result of that very supervision, are less often challenged to solve certain problems for themselves.[14]

The *resource dilution hypothesis*, similarly favored by evolutionary biologists, psychologists, and anthropologists, states that firstborn children—at least until the birth of the second—benefit from the undivided time, attention, and other "resources" that their parents "invest" in them. The second child can never count on the same luxury.

Then there's what an American sociologist calls the "fatigue effect": for parents with more than one child, subjected to multiple, often conflicting, demands, parenting ideals soon become more flexible.[15]

That effect could in part explain why Swedish parents, according to a group of economists studying their data, were less inclined to discuss homework and school performance with the second child than they had been with the first. The same data points to firstborns reading more books in their teens (yep!), and spending more time on their homework and less time watching TV and playing computer games than second and subsequent children.[16]

"Obviously," said a young American mother I know when I summed up these three hypotheses for her. She rolled her eyes.

My own reaction was less irritated: I felt uncomfortable, in fact, felt caught in the act. The theory confirmed my own experience, and did nothing to remove my unease about it.

○

When my son was almost one, we drove to France for our first holiday as a family of four. My notes from that time are mainly about my daughter, who was going through a demanding phase.

One moment she refused to walk, the next she ran away from us, only to stumble over tree roots and scream bloody murder; one moment she didn't feel like doing anything, the next she wanted to do all the things she wasn't yet capable of. One moment she was all sad and sorry for herself, the next cheerful and over-flowing with energy, chattering our ears off. At night she had nightmares, and in the mornings we were all exhausted.

During the day my partner and I took it in turns to nap. Whoever wasn't asleep tried to entertain my daughter, to calm her down or keep up with her. We had always been good at traveling, but now that there were four of us, the days seemed to crumble before our very eyes—which were often closed.

My son, meanwhile, lay for hours on end on a blanket in the grass and babbled at the trees. He was calm and easily satisfied. He demanded less than his elder sibling, and received less, because what we had to give was finite, our resources diluted indeed.

You might call that fair: each child got what they needed. But neither of the two got any more than that. And more was what I wanted for both of them.

○

To get it out of my system, I add one last study to my list on the birth-order effect. In 2016, the *Journal of Human Resources* published a study examining the data of almost five thousand US children and their parents. Here, too, the researchers saw that, on average, first children scored higher on cognitive tests and achieved better grades in school than second and subsequent children.[17]

Since the researchers also had access to data about the

parents, they were able to analyze what those parents did differently, the second (or third, or fourth) time.

All sorts of things, it emerged. They read less frequently to their second and subsequent children, undertook fewer activities tailored to the age of the youngest child, went on fewer cultural excursions, and took less time to educate their later-born children about fundamental concepts such as numbers, the alphabet, colors, and shapes than they had their elder siblings.

The parents offered their children, in the words of the researchers, a less "cognitively enriching environment" than they had created for their first children.[18] With the arrival of a second child, they wrote, the pressure on parents' attention and time increases. Under that pressure, parents may well choose to put the "non-essential" aspects of child-raising, such as cognitive development, on the back burner.[19]

(Parents did seem just as committed to the *emotional* development of their younger children as their elder ones. When time is scarce and you have to choose between comforting and reading aloud, reading aloud comes in second.)

In making that choice, the study concluded, parents put their second and later-born children "on a lower path for cognitive development and academic achievement, with lasting impact on adult outcomes."[20]

Say it ain't so, I think when I read that.

That evening I ask my son if he wants to read a story together. He's sitting on the sofa, leafing through a picture book about an owl chick that can't find its mother.

Enthusiastically, he waddles to the bookcase, picks up a book, and hands it to me. He sits down next to me and proceeds to continue flicking through his own book.

I guess you could call it reading together.

9

Time is a currency

Raising children costs time,
but whose time?

One muggy spring morning, my son, now one and a half, wakes up with one eye as big as a bull's testicle—red, swollen, and pressed shut. It makes his face curiously asymmetrical, like that of a small, good-looking Quasimodo, or the flawed yet sympathetic main character in a Martin Scorsese film. ("Wait till you see the other guy!" a neighbor cries enthusiastically when I step out the door with my son in my arms. We're on our way to the hospital.)

The cause of his newly acquired bad-guy look turns out to be a bacterial infection in his eye socket which, if not promptly treated, could also affect the rest of his eye. He's admitted for a course of antibiotics.

For two days and nights he stays in the hospital, that limbo, roaming the airtight rooms and corridors of the children's clinic. There's a playroom, a CliniClown,

and there are two pedagogical staff members ready to
tend to him with games, books, or whatever catches his
fancy.

For the most part, my son seems to view the entire episode as an interesting outing. When the drip is inserted,
he cries so hard he falls silent, his mouth wide open, just
gasping for breath. But once that's over, and half his arm
is in a splint to stop him from pulling the needle out
by himself, he seems immediately resigned to the new
situation. Life with one arm, another adventure.

That first night, I sleep next to him in the hospital ward.
Sea-green walls, a cheery orca on the bulletin board,
orange linoleum on the floor. He sleeps on his tummy,
buttocks in the air, a little hump of child. Twice the nurse
comes to connect the drip and disconnect it again; twice
he sleeps through it, beeps and pricks and all.

My own sleep is fleeting and broken. It puts me in
mind of the period when he'd just been born: I recognize
the half sleep, the vigilance, the stolen naps, five minutes
here, a quarter of an hour there. And how, in that state of
semislumber, certain thoughts begin to repeat themselves
and won't let go.

Here in the hospital, to my shame, my thoughts turn
out to be not just about him, but about myself as well.
About how I'm losing work time now; about how that certainly isn't something I should be worrying about; about
my apparent inability to put myself second. And again:
work time, priorities, selfishness, and so on.

I stand up, go over to stand by his bed, observe his profile.

His pursed lips form a beak, his cheek is round and soft, his surrender to sleep as uncomplicated as when he was a newborn.

○

Children are precious. Raising your offspring can cost you your freedom, your sleep, your money, and especially your time. Perhaps it's enough to say that parenthood costs time—time is money, when it comes down to it; freedom is the capacity to choose how you allocate your time; and sleep is one of the most time-consuming activities in life.

While expecting my son, I assumed that my second child would cost me as much time as my first. I suppose I also suspected I would have less time to spend on each child once I was a mother of two. But *how much* time does parenthood cost exactly? And how much extra does a second child require?

For decades now, sociologists and economists have taken it upon themselves to measure, categorize, and compare the demands children make on their parents' time. They do this by asking representative samples of parents how much time they have spent caring for their offspring in the past week. Or they get them to keep a diary for twenty-four hours, in which they note what they're doing every ten to fifteen minutes, and who is keeping them company.

From the second half of the twentieth century, many governments have systematically asked representative subsets of their citizenries to keep such diaries, among other things to get a sense of the kinds of work you don't find in statistics about the labor market: child-rearing, volunteer work, and informal care.

In the Netherlands, time diaries form the basis of many a report by the Netherlands Institute for Social Research (SCP). Since one minute in 1975 lasts precisely as long as one minute now, it's relatively easy to identify historical trends or compare different social groups, Anne Roeters, a family sociologist at the SCP, tells me. Relatively, because while one minute always lasts sixty seconds, the ways in which care and child-raising are defined can vary substantially across these studies.

Roeters gives me a reading list with titles of academic books and articles on the time children cost. One rainy day, I go and look them up, in a dimly lit library with dark red walls, where some compassionate soul has placed a packet of biscuits by the kettle.

There I learn that, in the neatly classifiable world of researchers, there's a distinction between primary care (feeding, changing, dressing, that kind of work), interactive care (reading aloud, playing, talking), and passive supervision (keeping an eye on your children while they play by themselves). In rebellious reality, these forms of care of course overlap.

There is also a category of "indirect care": all the extra time that children require of their parents due to longer shopping lists, more washing, more mess to tidy up, and more logistics.

Then there's the time when your children are elsewhere and you're engaged in other activities, but in principle you're still "available," on call. Caring for children, two sociologists note, is not only an activity but also a "state of mind,"[1] one that can't simply be captured in time diaries.

Indeed. While I read about these time allocations in the library twilight, I think constantly of my children. They were both tearful when I dropped them off at school and daycare that morning, and I'm still wondering how they're doing. I'm the one responsible for interrupting myself like this, but it feels like it's them doing it.

"That's right, go and blame the children," writes Anna Enquist in *Counterpoint*.[2]

Still, despite the different definitions and the sometimes artificial distinctions between the various types of care, most studies reveal comparable results. In almost all countries where researchers have looked into how much and what kind of time parents "invest" in their children, mothers spend more time on primary care than fathers.[3] In the Netherlands, as in many other countries, mothers spend more than twice as long on the physical care of children, such as washing and feeding, than fathers do. And almost everywhere, parents derive more pleasure from those other, less routine and less urgent forms of care, the interactive care, than from primary care.[4]

Moreover, the total quantity of time parents spend on

their children has changed in recent decades: how much time children cost turns out to be quite time-sensitive. And perhaps the same goes for how we *value* time.

○

When my son was four months old, he went to daycare for the first time. The same staff member who had enveloped my daughter in her arms two years earlier was there to welcome him. And although I could imagine no warmer destination, that day I cursed my job, the dual-income model, and my far-too-short maternity leave. I felt as though I was robbing him of my time—as if our time together was being taken from us.

I recognized the feeling: when I took his sister there for the first time, I also had the feeling that this initiation had come too soon, that something wasn't right about the system that "we" had "all" apparently agreed to.

But at least in her case I'd been able to give her all my time and attention in the four months leading up to that moment. My time with her little brother had been interrupted more often, and he'd had to share it with her. That made it feel all the more harsh, the second time.

○

In her now canonical essay, published in 1967, "Het onbehagen bij de vrouw" (Women's discontent), the Dutch feminist author Joke Smit wrote that upon becoming mothers, most women saw their world shrink to the walls of their home. Within that home, chaos prevailed, a state that had to be constantly and repetitively suppressed: "work" and "rest" were no longer distinguishable, and all a woman could do was look on patiently as the result of her labor was being "dismantled beneath her hands."

Although Smit found it "fascinating to watch and help children grow up," it seemed problematic to her that this activity took up "twelve hours a day, seven days a week."[5] If it were down to her, women would do the same as men: work, for a salary, outside the home. Their world would expand, their discontent shrink accordingly.

Since Smit published her essay, many mothers in industrialized countries have done precisely what she argued for: they have entered the labor market en masse. But, for many women, that has meant replacing one form of discontent—that of full-time care for small children—with another: the anxious suspicion that the time they put into their careers has been swiped from under their children's noses.

(It's crazy how fast such a cultural transformation can take place. "Maybe," says a friend expecting her first child, "maybe at the end of my maternity leave I just won't go back to work at all." She's the first from my circle of friends whom I've heard say such a thing, and for this she sounds tough, defiant, and daring.)

In 2000, the US sociologist Suzanne M. Bianchi published a study that upended the idea of working time as coming at a heavy cost to time for children. Based on time diaries from the United States, she showed that working mothers may spend slightly less time with their children than mothers who do no paid work outside the home, but also that the difference was a great deal smaller than you might expect. The impact on the children's well-being also turned out to be almost nonexistent.[6]

Bianchi offered a number of explanations for the limited impact mothers' participation in the labor market had on time with, and well-being of, children.

For one, it seems we may have overestimated how much time mothers previously spent with their children. Moreover, the shrinking of families means that more time can be spent per child.

Bianchi also noticed that working mothers tend to "protect" the time they have available for their children by cutting back on other activities. And, finally, fathers have begun to spend more time with their children—so that children on balance can still count on a good deal of "parental time."[7]

It might sound contradictory, writes Bianchi, but in the course of the twentieth century, the total amount of time that children spend in the company of their parents, whether on a dual income or not, has in fact *increased*.[8]

Researchers in other countries have come to the same conclusion.[9] A study of the amount of time parents in Canada, the United States, and a whole range of European countries spent on direct care for their children reveals that parenthood, in terms of time, became considerably more expensive between 1965 and 2012.[10] Pretty much everywhere in the past half century, parents have come to spend not less but *more* time with their children. From on average 54 minutes per day for mothers in 1965 to 104 minutes in 2012. And from 16 minutes for men in 1965 to 59 minutes in 2012.

The increase turns out to be higher in highly educated parents (123 minutes for mothers and 74 for fathers) than for those with a lower level of education (94 minutes for mothers, 50 for fathers). That could be, the researchers write, because "helicopter parenting"—with parents constantly hovering over their children, monitoring every aspect of their lives and making adjustments where possible—is practiced mainly by wealthier socio-economic classes.

Also, more highly educated parents often have more time to put into the care of their children, simply because they can afford it. They have the freedom to take Wednesday afternoon off, or to come home earlier if their children demand it.

(Of course, no major pandemics took place during these five decades. I wonder how the data would skew had the time frame been lengthened by another decade, incorporating that strange period in the spring of 2020, when parents and children in many parts of the world were suddenly forced to spend a lot more time at home, keeping each other company at all hours. In some ways, this period would feel like a throwback to a time when staying home was what mothers did as a matter of course. In other ways, it would be like peeking into a distant, science-fiction-like future, in which traditional divisions between men and women, between public and private, between "life" and "work," became upended, scrambled, and for some, almost nonexistent. These changes would, for the most part, be temporary, and often frustrating, but perhaps they might also show some of us that the way we did things wasn't set in stone; that we could allocate our time differently if we had to, and might keep on doing so once it was no longer required of us.)

In the Netherlands, the SCP reports, there was no significant statistical increase in the time that parents spent on children between 1975 and 2011. But—and this is important—there was no reduction either, despite the fact that women took on much more paid work in that period than ever before. Bianchi's reasoning, that parents somehow manage to protect the time with their children, must apply here too. The great popularity of part-time work among Dutch women is one expression of that; the fact that parents with children living at home have relatively little "free time" is another.[11]

It's not often that I feel comforted by statistics. Here, in this library, while my son is at daycare, I do.

Where do we find the time children cost? What do parents trade in to be able to pay for it?

The first, simple answer is sleep.[12] Leisure suffers as well: all those hours in cafés, city walks without a specific destination in mind, sleeping in until midmorning, and Sundays spent loafing around—they in part form the price you pay for parenthood.

All that was predictable enough, of course—and yet to me, as to many other parents, it came as a shock, this specific loss. "My privileged relationship with time has changed," writes Rachel Cusk in *A Life's Work*. Caring for a baby forms "a sort of serfdom, a slavery, in that I am not free to go."[13]

Free time—the freedom to allocate and experience your time as you please.

Besides sleep and leisure, parents trade in their paid work, as Bianchi also observed. We protect the time with our children, at least temporarily, by adjusting our working hours or working less—or by stopping completely for a while.[14]

And it's here that the most pronounced differences between fathers and mothers arise. Because, most of the time, it's women who cut down on work when children come along.

○

On that holiday in France, when my son was almost one, I met a Dutch mother with three blond children aged five to nine. She'd once had a flourishing practice as a dietician, and initially the self-employed life had combined nicely with care for her children.

But it was after the arrival of the third that it began to seem impracticable, keeping her business running on top of the business her family had become, on top of the organizing, the endless laundry, the back and forth to school and daycare.

"I would have to get to three different classrooms," she said with a pained expression, "wrap three children up in coats and scarves and hats and shoes." The whole exercise became so ridiculous, she said, that in the end she gave up her job completely.

Her husband, meanwhile, cheerfully continued working, a full forty hours a week.

Her story suggests that my question as to how much time a child costs, and how much time a second child adds on top of that, can almost always be answered with a counter-question: *whose time?*

Because if there's something sociologists, economists, and a great many parents constantly see confirmed, it's that mothers and fathers do not "pay" for parenthood in equal measure.

In the United States, for example, mothers spend around twice as much time with their children as fathers do, devoting on average 13.5 hours to childcare a week, compared to 7.3 hours for fathers, according to time-use data gathered by Pew Research in 2011.[15]

Things aren't much different in the Netherlands. The SCP reports not only that mothers spend more time than fathers on the physical care of their children; they spend more time on their children overall. In 2016, mothers spent on average 9.9 hours a week caring for their children (aged under eighteen and living at home), compared with 6 hours for fathers. For mothers, 6.1 of those hours went to physical care and bedtime routines; 3.8 hours went to supervisory activities such as helping with homework, playing, and reading aloud. Fathers clocked 2.8 hours in the first category and 3.1 in the second.

Nine point nine and six point one hours per week: for people with children, that doesn't sound like very much. And it's not; this tally included only those moments in which caring for children constituted the "main" or "secondary" activity. The hours in which parents were doing something other than caring or supervising but were still in their children's company—over dinner, for instance, or on an outing to a museum—aren't accounted for. Ask Dutch parents about *all* the time they spend with their children, and for fathers you come to almost thirty hours per week, compared with almost forty for mothers.[16]

That difference in time allocation is reflected in the distribution of paid work: pretty much all over the world, fathers work outside the home more than mothers. In the Netherlands the difference is around eighteen hours per week. There seems to be "a kind of 'exchange' of paid and unpaid work within families," is how the SCP pus it.[17] (Besides spending more time on care and supervision of children, mothers also spend more time on housework.)

An exchange. It sounds so businesslike, so cold, for something that in practice feels more like an unreasoned, more or less spontaneous manner of cohabitation. Yet that exchange is one of the reasons why the decision of whether to have a second child is sometimes cast as an economic choice: the more children a woman has, the greater the "gap" in her résumé and the greater the impact on her future income.[18]

That's why sociologists and economists speak of a "motherhood penalty": the disadvantage that mothers experience on the labor market compared to women without children. The penalty is greater the bigger the batch of children grows. A Danish study published in 2018 points out that, compared with childless women, working mothers with two children experience a bigger reduction in their income than working mothers of just one child. Mothers of three and four experience a further drop, whereas the income of fathers is hardly even dented, however many children they have.[19]

A penalty, or an exchange? In any case: if time is a currency, then the exchange rate isn't the same for everyone, men and women don't pay with the same coinage, and not every child is equally expensive.

○

Two children cost their parents more time than one. That makes sense if you take in the long view—when a person has a second child, that automatically adds a number of extra years of care, a couple of years longer until the last one leaves the nest. But in that hot summer in which I was pregnant with my son, I'd wondered whether the care for two children would also cost more time *per day*.

Not quite so much, it turns out. According to studies I've found on the subject, having a second child costs parents between six minutes and an hour extra per day.[20] The

Netherlands Institute for Social Research (SCP) discerns no significant difference between the time it costs to care for one child and that for two. After all, the family sociologist Anne Roeters speculates when I tell her about my surprise at this finding, most parents with two children care for them *simultaneously*. "You don't take your eldest child to daycare first, then cycle home to get the youngest," is how she explains it.

The time parents spend on their children therefore doesn't double when a second child comes along. And that's precisely what lies at the foundation of what economists call the "dilution" of parent-child time. Time is scarce, so the more children you have, the less time remains available *per child*.[21]

That dilution doesn't affect all children to the same extent, several studies show. For instance, research into parent-child time among British families showed that first children tended to receive more parental time than second or subsequent children.[22] And economists who analyzed time diaries by more than 3,000 US families saw that second children on average had to make do with 3.5 hours less "quality time" per week from their mother than first children at the same age. Third children received 4.5 hours less quality time per week from their mother.[23]

Researchers also found that parents tend to allocate the time differently when a second child comes along. In a study from the United States, for instance, I read that mothers of two or more children, compared with mothers of just one, spend more time on "passive supervision" and less on interactive care.[24] They will, for example, watch while their children run around in the snow more often than read to them or play with them. (Of course, this was also what emerged from one of those studies of the relationship between birth order and cognitive skills: that parents read to and taught their second child less than they had the first.)

One possible interpretation is that the children play *together* and so don't need their mother as much. Another, it occurs to me after I've been examined in the mirror by a pale specter with bags under her eyes, is that mothers of one child have more energy left to really interact with their child.

Children cost time, lots of time. But what that means in practice depends on where you stand. Children currently cost more parental time than they used to, they cost mothers more than fathers, and the way fathers and mothers allocate their time also differs. To a certain extent, work time and time with children are communicating vessels, but parents draw on other reserves as well. And although I have the feeling that my children, now that there are two of them, take up more time than when only the first was with us, the statistics tell a different story. On paper, caring for two children barely costs more time than caring for one.

That last point, the modest increase in daily caring time when a second child comes along, leads me to suspect that the arrival of the second child has more of an influence on the nature and intensity of parent-child time than on its quantity. The second child influences not only parental time allocation, but the way in which parents perceive time as well.

And in order to understand how *that* works, I need to look somewhere completely different—not at the objective minutes and hours of sociologists and economists, but at the often terribly contradictory ways in which we ourselves experience time.

10

Long days, short years
How children transform time

In the winter, when my son was a year old, we moved to a new, more practically partitioned apartment on the other side of the river. It was cold and rainy, and by the time we'd unpacked the last of the boxes, a snowstorm came along. The daycare called, asking us to collect our children early so that the staff could get home on time; most of them lived farther out, in the next village or town. They were dependent on the train or bus and didn't want to get snowed in.

The traffic throughout the city center was gridlocked, so my partner arrived rather late anyway. I was standing waiting at the window when they got home; it was already dark out. That evening, the four of us went outside to make a snowman in the square next to our new house. This involved putting on snowsuits and winter boots and hats and gloves and scarves. It took an eternity to get out of the house, and it struck me as out of bounds, the number of actions that had to be completed before we could even get started.

Once in the square, my son took two cautious steps in the snow, which reached above his knees. It was dark and silent and somehow reminded me of the past, of my own childhood. I looked at him and tried to get the memory clear—it had something to do with what it felt like to wear a snowsuit like that, how it restricted your freedom of movement but also made you feel safe. I didn't get long to think about it: my son looked around him, took a deep breath, and wanted to go back indoors. Expedition Snowman hadn't even properly begun, and already he was done with it.

I lifted him up the steps, undid his scarf, pulled his gloves off and then his hat, unclipped his snow boots, and peeled off his suit. Everything hung over the radiator, ready for the next round.

A pool of water accumulated on the floor beneath.

○

A minute lasts a minute. You can compare fathers' minutes with mothers' minutes, you can count up the minutes that children cost altogether, and you can look at where parents get those minutes from.

But that tells us nothing about how such a minute *feels*. Time perception is more slippery, harder to capture in statistics and lists than its objective duration.

Nevertheless, the way children transform how time feels is at least as fundamental. And that's what I want to know: how do we experience time, as parents? And to what extent does that experience change when a second child comes along?

"With children," a friend remarked a couple of years ago, "days are long and years are short." It was summer then, and we were in New York; our first child was one and a half and our second not yet born. We were walking along the Hudson, my friend, my partner, and I, while our daughter slept in the stroller.

I already knew then what she meant, and now, years later, now that we have a second child, I understand it even better.

For at least half a century, social scientists have been trying to map out what parenthood does *to parents*. How it affects their well-being, for instance, their relationship, their work. And parents, when asked about the most important change that having a child brings, always talk about *one* thing in particular: time.

"New fathers and mothers," a psychologist wrote in the early 1980s when taking stock of research into the transition to parenthood, "report that sleep time, television time, communication time, sex time, and even bathroom time are all in short supply, thanks to their newborns. Paradoxically, they also say that they are more often bored."[1]

Parents are short of time, and yet they have too much of it—days are long and years are short.

It's what neuropsychologists call the "classic time paradox." How you perceive time depends very much on the moment. In a "prospective" assessment of time, you estimate the duration of an event *while it's still in progress*. A "retrospective" assessment is made afterward—and very different processes come into play in the two different modes.

Take feeding a baby, for example: it lasts forever when you're doing it (prospective). The same goes for repeatedly reading the same book to a child or going through the motions between dinner and bedtime. The actions are repetitive and predictable; there is little that's new, so boredom can strike at any moment—and days are long.

But if you look back later (retrospective), there often isn't much you remember from such episodes—and as a result the entirety melts away, reduced to almost nothing. Details don't stick, and years are short.

I noticed the same thing on that brief foray into the snow: that now that we have a second child, a much greater share of my time is taken up with repetition and routine than it used to be. My children may not cost me any *more* time now, than before, but the allocation of that time really has changed.

I seem to be permanently occupied tying scarves, zipping up snowsuits, waiting until one is ready to go, chasing after the other, running back up the stairs because one of them has forgotten something, just needs one last pee, or suddenly has an acute hankering for something or other. They're all actions I've performed a hundred times before and *seem* as if they're preparatory in nature, but they often end up being the entire activity.

("If there's *one* category that directly experiences 'vanitas vanitatum,'" writes Joke Smit, "it's that of mothers with small children."[2] And yes, sometimes it does feel like the ultimate exercise in futility.)

Could it be those many routine, preparatory actions that lead nowhere that cause me to perceive time as moving more slowly, as if it's more syrupy in texture, than when it was just my daughter? The fiddling with coats and hats in winter, I mean, with sunscreen in summer, endless repetitions that take up so much more of my time now that there are two of them? And is that why that same syrupy time, in retrospect, seems to have flown by?

○

It's spring, and my son's already walking and has started naming the world around him out loud, when the girl next door gives my daughter a watch as a gift. It's pink, with a picture of Minnie Mouse on its face, and it doesn't work—but that doesn't matter, my daughter can't tell the time yet anyway; in fact, she has only a rudimentary notion of "time" at all. She probably also perceives time differently from me—less compartmentalized, less like a thing to be measured, won or lost. Not something you're more or less always aware of, somehow or other, that you take into account, whatever you do.

And I hope she can remain this innocent for a long

time to come, this free of everything we, her parents, already think we know about time.

She wants to know what time it is—two on her watch, five on the kitchen clock.

"Two o'clock," I say.

"Look," she says proudly. "When I want to make time go faster, all I have to do is press this button." The hands whirl around from two o'clock to half past two, to three, to half past three—in no time.

○

Newborn babies, with their idiosyncratic rhythms, tend to throw their parents' time perception completely out of whack. Not only do they render meaningless the difference between day and night; they change the contours of time, depriving it of continuity.

"The days with the baby felt long but there was nothing expansive about them," observes the narrator of Jenny Offill's novel *Dept. of Speculation*: "Caring for her required me to repeat a series of tasks that had the peculiar quality of seeming both urgent and tedious. They cut the day up into little scraps."[3] Time is no longer a stream the course of which you can adjust yourself, but becomes something that feels simultaneously imposed from outside, and taken from you.

Even after those first, sleepless weeks, time tends to remain fragmented and somewhat dispossessed. "The children were small and enthralling," the main character of Anna Enquist's *Counterpoint* recalls, looking back on the early years with her two children: "At any moment she had to . . . be ready to leap up to get a drink, something to read to them, answer a question."[4]

Two children, I now know, each fragment your time in their own way. When my son had just been born, his rhythm constantly clashed with that of his elder sister. The chaos of that early beginning has now died down, but there are still days that I spend with them where I feel like a ridiculous puppet, controlled by not one but two puppet masters. Dictatorial, sardonic puppet masters they are, who swing me back and forth, and sometimes pull me in two directions at once. The effect then, too, is that time moves agonizingly slowly, yet there's also never enough of it.

In the novel *Faces in the Crowd,* by Valeria Luiselli, the narrator observes that novelists always say that novels "need a sustained breath." She has two children: "They don't let me breathe. Everything I write is—has to be—in short bursts. I'm short of breath."[5]

(Properly inhaling and exhaling once takes around three seconds, the neuropsychologist Marc Wittmann reports in *Felt Time*. Coincidentally or not, two to three seconds is also approximately the length of time for which most of us perceive "now"—the duration of a "moment." And, researchers have discovered, it's also the length of sounds exchanged by mothers and babies.[6])

"These are the intense years," my partner and I regularly tell each other. "It'll get easier later on." What we mean by "easier" is that we hope our children will take up less and less of our time. Or in any case, that they won't always require this endless routine, will stop hacking our time into pieces.[7]

"Those darling children who eat all my time," Zadie Smith once wrote.[8] That's how I experience it as well, especially now that I have two. More often than I'd like, I have the paradoxical feeling that those people I've intentionally brought into the world, and who are so dear to me, for whom I'd give my life, are the very people out to take something that's "mine."

For centuries, the passage of time was something you noticed by the work you'd done, the changing seasons, the position of the sun. Then along came clocks, and time became standardized; we began to count it. Since then, time has often been thought of as a currency: it's "ours," we can "spend," "waste," or "invest" it; we can "keep it to ourselves" or "give it away"—and it can be "taken" from us.

But since our second child arrived, that metaphor has increasingly struck me as misguided. Although I can quite often choose how I spend my time—where I focus my attention at a given moment, where I go or who I'm with—at least as often, I have no say in it at all. That's because two unpredictable factors—small children—have burrowed their way into my life, and in all their innocence have dictated to me how I spend my time. Their wishes, their pace, and their need for repetition largely determine what we do with our time as a family, and how I feel about it.

○

I regularly look back on that feverish night with my son in the hospital. Perhaps because that episode illustrated so well how, precisely in the moments when a child throws your schedule out the window, time ceases to be a currency you can spend at will.

Time becomes something else in those moments: more mysterious, less comprehensible. More, perhaps, as it was in the past, in a mythical era, before we had railways, clocks, and conveyor belts, before Minnie Mouse watches even existed. Time becomes something that happens to you, and with which you can't do much other than experience it.

In her book *Valuing Children*, the American economist Nancy Folbre proposes that we conceive of the relationship between parents and children not in terms of the "investments" that parents make in their offspring but of the "commitments" they have made to them. I read this one Friday afternoon in the university library; my partner's home with the children, so I can stay until closing time.

And though such a concept seems blindingly obvious to me, at the same time it sounds pleasantly refreshing. I suppose it's because the work of economists and sociologists and evolutionary biologists often strikes me as so calculating. The work of those, I mean, who analyze the relationship between parental time investments and "child outcomes" as if they were talking about production processes, or as if the family were a factory. In goes time and out come IQs and other test scores. Or who describe the time you spend on your children as a parent as an "opportunity cost." After all, you could have done something else with that time: made money, for instance.[9]

In light of that view of parents and children, Folbre's proposal is not only refreshing; it's almost radical. A commitment, she writes, is a promise that remains binding, even when the expected "return on investment" remains absent. In contrast with an investment, moreover, a commitment brings with it moral duties—duties that you can't just dispose of if the "results" are disappointing.[10]

In the moments when time ceases to be "mine"— when it no longer feels like an individual possession or a currency—it takes on, for me at least, the nature of that kind of commitment.

That was what happened in the hospital, while my son was asleep and I stood by his bed. After my protestations and indignation, and my shame at those protestations and indignation, I found acceptance. I stopped watching the clock and looked only at my son.

In such moments, time is more like a shared environment: it's no longer a resource to be diluted or divided but a common good, a shared place or space to which everyone in our tiny tribe has access. An environment that belongs to the community as a whole, and which my children and I are part of.

Within that environment, I can see our relationship not as revolving around the "investments" I make in them—time investments, which may or may not work out to be big enough or fair enough. When I perceive time in that way, I no longer need to be grudging or possessive, no longer need to feel like I'm coming up short.

Instead, we're defined by the way we're bound to one another, a collective, entangled and interdependent.

In such moments, I see our relationship as one based on the promise I've made, before they were even with us, and without fully understanding what it meant, that this is *our* time.

The siren song of the easy baby

On whether we have children
and how many

In the summer my son turns two, we go on holiday to Italy. We leave one sultry morning, during a seemingly endless heat wave. It's still dark out, and in the half-light all the sounds—closing doors, clicking seat belts—seem louder and more intense than usual. All four of us talk more quietly in compensation.

The children are sitting in the back seat, a bag of provisions between them, each with a thumb in their mouth. On our way, my son points out windmills, cranes, and electricity pylons. He only recently discovered the difference: previously, all large structures were windmills to him, and he would greet them enthusiastically, like a sort of inverse Don Quixote. Now his vocabulary has expanded, and I imagine that this means he has a more granular view of things as well.

When they sleep, I take photos—my son's full lips, my daughter's wonderful poses. I take photos because I suspect that this, turning around in a passenger seat to find two sleeping children, is an experience I'll otherwise forget.

Thirty years ago, my parents must have looked around in the same way, at me and my sister, on a highway traveling south, while it gradually became light outside. And as is often the case of late, I'm overcome with the sensation that I'm following a script from my childhood. Except that now I'm playing a different role—not that of the child but that of the mother, not in the back seat but in front.

That week we sleep in a big tent on a small campsite, where three other families, all Italian, are on holiday as well. Each of the three families has one child: a boy of eight, a boy of six, and a girl of two, with big, anime-style eyes, onto whom my daughter immediately latches. Compared with those modest, nimble Italian units, our pack feels large, lively, and loud.

At the next campsite, it's a different story. We've driven to the foot of the Alps and now find ourselves among other Dutch families, who without exception have two or three children each.

We're instantly back to average. Parents with three children, I once heard my mother say, "they're the real pros."

Two is the norm. My partner and I have joined the crowd— because we could, because we wanted our daughter to have a sibling, and because we, or in any case I, wanted to experience the spectacle one more time.

It's also possible that we longed to reproduce the family dynamics we knew from our own childhoods: a family with two children in my case, three in my partner's, in both cases more than one.

I assumed that these were personal motivations, complemented by fluke, good luck: we were fertile and our children were healthy. Not once did it occur to me that there might be *other* reasons why we wanted and in fact were able to become a standard family.

But the idea that our preferences came into being autonomously was largely an illusion—as the idea of autonomy probably always is. Whether we have children, and if so, how many, has everything to do with what happens outside the walls of our potential family homes.

Just before we left for Italy, I'd immersed myself in demographic developments in Europe. I already knew, therefore, that Italy's fertility rate is at a historic low: 1.4 children per woman on average.

This is not so much because a relatively large number of Italian women remain childless, or because large families are less common. No, the most important reason is that Italian mothers, compared with mothers from countries with higher birth rates, more often stop at one.

"Missing children of birth order two," wrote three

economists in 2017, contribute the most to the difference in birth rates between countries with "low fertility," such as Italy, and countries with a relatively "high fertility," such as the Netherlands, where the birth rate is around 1.7.

"Missing children of birth order two"—it sounds like a premise for a thriller or crime series. In actual fact, if I am to believe these authors, it's a matter of policy. For those missing second children are not a reflection of changing ideals; in Italy, as elsewhere in Europe, most people favor a two-child family—which means that some Italian parents have fewer children than they would really like. According to the economists who wrote the paper, this has to do with, among other things, childcare being relatively expensive and inaccessible.[1]

Italy's missing second children suggest that the choice for a second or even a third child is determined not only by individual desires, longings, and opportunities but also by external circumstances—institutional provision, the state of the economy, gender norms, and so on.

I had also read a paper about Icelandic fathers who took paternity leave after the birth of their first child—since the year 2000, Iceland has had a generous paternity leave program in place, with at least three months of paid leave. The researchers wanted to know to what extent this program influenced the decision to have no children, one child, or more. Their conclusion: compared with fathers who hadn't taken their leave after their first child was born, those who did take leave were much more likely to have a second child. Or, as the authors of the paper formulated it, fathers who took leave faced a significantly higher "second-birth risk."[2]

The explanation: fathers on paternity leave tend to take on a larger proportion of housework and caring tasks, and the more equal the division of labor at home, the easier it is for mothers to combine care and paid work. This "makes the decision to have another child easier," the researchers claim.

The conclusion sounds plausible, but it was that one word—"risk"—that stuck with me. It put me in mind of our discussions back when we still had only one child, of how my partner hadn't been particularly interested in having a second and how intolerable I became as a result. He primarily saw risk in what I wanted, and perhaps it was the contrast between his interpretation and mine of the same phenomenon that most enraged me, most made me weep. It was the fact that we were looking at the same thing but seeing something different: I found it maddening.

In another study, examining more than 7,500 British families, a researcher looked into the relationship between the characteristics of the first child and the parents' decision to have a second. The article displayed graphs reflecting the likelihood of having a second child in what was apparently termed a "hazard function." One such figure showed that the risk of a second child, the second-child hazard, increases along with the first child's scores on cognitive and social-emotional skills.[3] In other words, the second-child hazard increases when the first is an "easy" child.

I picture my son, all thirty pounds of him, thundering toward the sharp edge of a bookcase. In the world of parents, it's the bookcase that forms a hazard. In the world of the Finnish social epidemiologist who conducted this study, it's the arrival of the second child.

A colleague kindly pointed out to me that terms such as "risk" and "hazard" are very common in economic and demographic circles, that they're no less neutral than, say, "chance" or "tendency." I shouldn't read too much into it, she said.

But the words we use shape our view of things. (Or maybe our view of things shapes how certain words make us feel.) And I can't help but hear something accusatory in this relationship between parental leave and the "risk" of a second birth. As if the parents have been set up, as if they could have escaped—if only they hadn't fallen into the trap of paternity leave. And that easy first child who increases the hazard of a second—it reads as if the first child manipulated her parents with her good behavior.

(Of course, no amount of good behavior can outdo the pressure of major outside forces. Four years after the publication of that study on paternity leave and second-birth "hazard," the world would be in the throes of a pandemic, parents and children would suddenly be spending a lot more time together, and the experience of parenthood would change profoundly for many of us. "If there's a baby boom in 9 months," reads a tweet going viral during this time, "it'll consist entirely of first-born children.")[4]

○

In Italy, among the Dutch holidaymakers, my daughter asks if there'll be another baby, a third. We're sitting in the tent, and I'm rubbing sunscreen onto my children, as I do every morning. The eldest endures the process with resignation; the youngest protests.

"Another baby?" I ask. "You mean another little brother or sister?"

My daughter nods.

I ask her why she would want that. "I'd want to help you," she says, "and care for that baby."

I say she's already helping us now, isn't she?

But she'd like to do "more difficult things," she says.

She wants to change diapers, prepare bottles, and carry out other tasks for which her brother is now too big, wants to help with things he no longer needs.

I can't come up with an answer right away. The answer to the question of why you might want children in the first place is complicated enough. The answer to the question of how you actually get around to having them is many times more complex.

Many of the reasons for having a second child are less idiosyncratic than I once thought. The desire for a baby, curiosity about parenthood, the wish to give a first child a sibling, and genetic luck all play a role. But so do the state of the economy, job security, provisions such as paternity leave and subsidized childcare. Not to mention cultural stereotypes about only children, and whether your first baby is an easy one.

They're factors that, consciously or subconsciously, enter into the way we reproduce. Those factors make choices possible or rule them out, suggest options, conceal others.

Then of course there's another factor, one I haven't come across in studies involving Icelandic fathers or Italian mothers, but which parents around me talk about with increasing frequency. It's a factor that may well be the most fundamental of all, but that's also the hardest to take into account when considering having a first, second, or third child.

In the weeks leading up to our holiday, the newspapers published daily stories about how extremely hot summers like this one stood to become the new normal. The cause of this global warming is us, humans. If we continue on our current path, generations to come will have to deal with extreme weather conditions and a lack of resources—and, in the cautionary words of the philosopher Sarah Conly, they will be left with "lives vastly inferior to our own, if they are able to eke out a living at all."[5]

And while fertility rates in wealthy industrialized countries have gone down in recent decades, the world population continues to grow larger. In many countries, mothers still have more than two children: the summer we were in Italy, the world population was up to 7.6 billion, with 2.4 children born for every woman.[6]

That's less than the 4.7 of half a century ago, but more than the 2.1 needed to keep the population steady. Conly argues that, at least in the prosperous, industrialized parts of the world, people ought to get a grip. That they should have no children, or if parenthood is a precondition for a fulfilled life, they should have no more than one.

Conly belongs to a growing group of philosophers, journalists, and activists who are in favor of birth restriction for the sake of the planet. In the year my son was born, an international group of researchers published a book in which they calculated the potential impact of different climate solutions. High on their list was better family planning, in combination with more education for girls. The decreasing birth rate that would result from this would bring about a greater drop in CO_2 emissions than all the windmills imaginable put together.[7]

Just before my son's first birthday, a report came out in which climate scientists predicted that if a US family chose to put one fewer child into the world than was initially the plan, it would save as much in carbon dioxide emissions as 684 teenagers deciding to recycle everything that could be recycled for the rest of their lives.[8]

"Want to Fight Climate Change? Have Fewer Children" was the headline in *The Guardian*. Other newspapers and magazines hurled out headlines in a similar spirit:

"Should We Be Having Children in the Age of Climate Change?"

"How Do You Decide to Have a Baby When Climate Change Is Remaking Life on Earth?"

"One Child Less Than I Want"

And yet. And yet my partner and I had children. Sometimes we tell each other there's still a chance that things will genuinely be better in the future, more pleasant, cleaner, and more sustainable. That those who have children have faith.

"Having children," as a friend who is also a mother once put it, "is an act of hope."

In the tent I try to grab hold of my son so I can put sunscreen on him too. All holiday he's refused to wear a T-shirt, running around bare-chested instead. His skin is brown, smooth—he's still "really dark"—but his hair is turning increasingly blond.

He runs from me giggling, looking over his shoulder to see if I've understood the game and am coming after him.

He bangs into the table leg and bursts into tears.

It occurs to me that we don't so much have children because we're hopeful as the other way around: if you have children, you have to look to the future. Once our children are with us, we have no choice other than to hope for a leap in progress: for policy and mentality changes big enough to call a halt to further warming, and to learn to live with the consequences of the damage we've already wrought.

"I don't think so," I say to my daughter, who's still looking at me questioningly.

Then I go to my son, lift him up, and start comforting.

Epilogue

On expectations

Me: But tell me, what's it *really* like, being a second child?

My sister: Come on, that's a personal question disguised as a general question.

Me: OK. What's it like having me as an elder sister?

My sister: Not always easy. Not in the past anyway.

Me (although I already know the answer): Why not?

My sister: You never let me play with you. You could do so much more than me. And when I started high school, all the teachers said, "Ah, Lynn's little sister." They had high expectations. But I already knew I could never fulfill them.

○

I didn't have children yet when I read Lydia Davis's story "What You Learn About the Baby," in which the narrator describes the first weeks with a child in brief, note-like passages.[1] She writes that, as a new mother, you learn to make your bed right away, because it won't get a look-in later in the day, and sums up the kinds of questions a child can invoke—for instance, how his mouth knows it's a mouth, "when it imitates yours."

And she writes about the "dark grey lint" that gathers in the lines of her baby's little hands, those clammy little hands that almost always form a fist in the early days, making them the ideal place for dirt to settle.

Not long after my first child was born, I too saw that lint in her little hands, and picked it out. Two and a half years later, once again, I opened my son's clenched fist to remove the fluff.

And I wonder: would I have seen that lint if I hadn't read about it beforehand? And if so, would it have been as satisfying, even without the special combination of anticipation and recognition, without the reward of a fulfilled expectation? What would have happened to that dirt, I mean, had I not expected it?

○

A couple of years ago, a group of developmental psychologists offered an additional explanation for the fact that second children, on average, perform less well in school than firstborn children.

Their study built on the work of economists,

psychologists, and biologists, who had previously demonstrated that parents distributed their time unevenly between first and second children and that the way time was allocated worked out differently for each child, as well. These same scientists also pointed out that from the get-go second children grow up in a different family than first children.

The additional explanation formulated in the new study, when I allowed it to sink in, was fairly heartrending.

The researchers had studied 388 families with two children, now teenagers. They had asked the parents if their children did well in school, and also, who did better. They then compared the parents' answers with the children's grades.[2]

As it turned out, most parents believed that their first child was the better student—*even when the first child didn't actually achieve better grades.*[3]

It's not the only study in which parents offer different estimations of their first- and second-borns: US researchers who scrutinized data from a national survey saw that mothers were more inclined to describe their first children as "one of the best students in the class," while second and later-born children were more likely to be assigned to "below the middle" or "near the bottom of the class."[4]

It may be the case, the researchers speculated, that parents have higher expectations of their first children. (It may be the case, I thought in irritation when I read that, that those expectations are in part inspired by piles and piles of academic and popular publications stating that firstborns, on average, perform better in school than second-borns.)

But they weren't yet finished with their explanation. It could be, they continued, that parents had a "higher" estimation of their first children because, compared with the second, they had long been operating at a higher level—already drawing princesses when the second was just scribbling all over the paper, already doing sums when the second was still learning to count.

Whatever the cause, the study pointed out that parents' uneven expectations had an impact in the real world. Because although children's school grades barely affected their parents' views of their performance, the reverse did show an effect: if parents assumed that their children differed in capabilities, the differences in school performance of those children really did grow bigger over time.

"When parents believed one child was more capable than the other, that child's school grades improved more over time than their sibling's," the researchers wrote.[5]

It was a self-fulfilling prophecy.

○

An expectation is a belief that something will happen. Expectations come in all shapes and sizes. There are expectations based on implicit knowledge or statistical probabilities, for instance, as well as expectations based on explicit knowledge about certain people and events. There are expectations on which we base conscious decisions, and expectations that shape us more or less by accident.

An example of the latter category is the stereotype effect, whereby people who are told that "people like them" (women, for example, or minorities) generally don't perform very well on a certain test, then go on to do worse on that test. Or take the Pygmalion effect, which arises when the high expectations teachers have for their pupils positively affect those pupils' academic performance.[6]

Or think of the placebo effect, which swings into action when a patient expects a pill to alleviate their pain and really does experience less pain as a result of that expectation, even when the pill doesn't contain much more than sugar. Doctors have known of the existence of this effect for centuries, though they've had different names for it: in a psychology textbook dating back to 1787, it was described as the "impact of imagination on the body."[7]

Many a parent gratefully makes use of it, this impact of imagination on the body. When I kiss my son's knee after a fall, or repeat an incantation with my daughter to ward off bad dreams, I create an expectation in my children—and that expectation *does something*.

Of course, that's not all I do in such moments: I comfort, I connect, I acknowledge. But still, it seems to me that expectation management is one of the main activities of parenthood.

Our expectations influence our perception in all kinds of ways. For instance, when we see what we expect to see and fail to notice what we don't expect. Think of that famous experiment in which participants are shown a video clip of a basketball game and are asked to concentrate and count how often the ball is passed between players.

Participants don't expect a gorilla to appear on the scene halfway through—and half of them *don't see it when it does*.

Expectations determine what we see and believe, and ultimately even our behavior—not to mention the behavior of those around us. In the study in which parents thought their eldest children were cleverer than their second children, those children were *shaped* by their parents' expectations. Parents had different expectations of each child, and so each child turned out different too.[8]

○

Two years ago, I found myself expecting for the second time. Only then did I see the many layers to that term. Expecting: we *expect* a child, in the sense that we await their arrival, that we believe they will be born; but we also expect a *child*, in the sense that we have ideas, assumptions, however vague, as to who that child will be—and who we, as parents, will be.

But what is the basis for your expectations, thoughts, and feelings about your children? Is it what you know about those children themselves—or is it what you *think* you know?

I think back to the parenting course I attended. How the instructor tried to explain to us that if you tell your eldest often enough how smart she is, or how responsible, or how helpful, that she'll come to see that as her identity, her role, as an expectation she has to meet. And that if your youngest hears often enough how brave and tough he is, he'll think that's how he should be, that there's no other option.

One mother, who always called her youngest son a "little rascal," turned red in the face.

Another, who had described her daughter earlier in the day as "sensitive" and her son as "more stable," felt a pang of guilt.

What I'm beginning to understand, slower than I'd like, is that the "knowledge" we think we have—the expectations we cherish with respect to our children, expectations that give us the illusion of predictability and control—is capable of trapping our children, or denting them. That our convictions have the capacity to close doors for our children, make particular paths unpassable, exclude options.

○

"Beautiful!" my son shouts, when I heave him for the umpteenth time into his sister's frayed princess dress.

"Beautiful!" I echo.

Two years ago, when my daughter began to wear dresses like this, my enthusiasm was less straightforward, more ambivalent. In her desire to be pretty, I thought I spied the beginning of a preoccupation with beauty, the opening salvo of a development that begins with princess dresses and ends with an eating disorder.

At heart, his budding love for synthetic, shiny, flowing clothes probably isn't any different from hers at the time: dress, beautiful, end of story. Typical of me, to see something taboo-breaking in his case, or at least a departure from the norm—and to derive satisfaction from that fact.

That the dress has taken on a different meaning now that our second child is wearing it is down to me. It's a projection: I look at my children, but I see myself.

○

Where do our ideas on parenthood come from? What about our ideas on parenting first and second children, and on growing up with a sibling?

There are books and online forums; there are conversations with the exhausted parents in our circles of friends. There are memories of our own childhoods, the images we have of our parents, our opinions of our own brothers or sisters.

And there are the articles of folk wisdom, the popular truths that seem to float through the ether and that you can pluck out at precisely the moment you need them. Truisms and clichés—about "your place in the family" and "what it does to you," for instance, or the amount of time and attention parents should ideally spend on their children.

On a foundation made up of all those sources, we erect our ideas, our expectations of how things will work out for our children—and ourselves.

Sometimes we can be told something a thousand times without understanding it, only for it to sink in on repetition one thousand and one. Somewhere between that parenting course and my son's discovery of princess dresses, it started to dawn on me.

That what I expected and feared for my second child had to do with how I saw my own relationship with my sister—a relationship that for a long time was badly skewed, full of conflict, and in which I suspected she'd drawn the short straw.

That it had to do, too, with one hundred and fifty years of birth order research. With the stubborn theories of Sigmund Freud, with the obsessions of Charles Darwin, with my own desire for predictability and knowability. With books and articles and other parents' stories, about other children.

What it had nothing to do with, or in any case very little, was with my second child himself.

○

It's impossible to approach parenthood as a blank slate. The second time around we certainly didn't manage it, if only because repetition always comes with expectations, or because the increased routine can crowd out the sense of wonder.

But that's not to say that I can't try, each time anew, not to tell my child's story in advance.

To forget the stories I know as much as possible.

And then do nothing but look and listen.

For instance at how, when you've just learned to walk, you stumble toward a low step, throw your toy frog on the ground, lie down flat on your tummy, and descend backward—as if climbing down a ravine, with all the circumspection that requires.

At how you look at your sister when she dances, and then run over to her, stand in front of her, and reach out your hands until she holds them. How proudly you look around you then.

At how you go up to the slide, squealing with laughter, slide down, stand up, and quickly run back to the steps, before anyone else can slide down and before I can lift you up to take you home. The joy of repetition, again and again and again and again, that must never be interrupted.

At how you sit on the sofa with a book of children's stories, and when I ask you if I can read it to you, you shake your head no. How you then turn your back on me so that I can't even *touch* the book. How you start hurriedly turning the pages, reading to yourself in a language that only you understand.

How you sit in your car seat, behind me in the back seat, on the long drive to Italy. How I reach my hand back and you take hold of it, and begin to stroke yourself with it, precisely the way you like: face, tummy, thigh, and again. And again.

I know I'll forget this, and that there's so much more that I've already long forgotten.

But perhaps forgetting is also a form of letting go, of making space, it occurred to me recently, when the three of us were walking across the schoolyard, hand in hand in hand. You were in the middle. A strange admixture of terror, pain, and delight welled up in me. And I knew at that moment, I needed nothing other than this: the giggling of two small persons who were in my belly once and now lived with me and my partner, and who would one day make their homes elsewhere.

But who were with us for now—and with each other.

Afterword and further reading

I wrote *Second Thoughts* by watching, but also by reading, perhaps more than I should have. I kept on coming back to certain books, and I warmly recommend them to anyone who would like to immerse themselves further in the subject.

In *A Natural History of Families* (Princeton University Press, 2005), behavioral ecologist Scott Forbes explains clearly and entertainingly how and why the interests of family members are sometimes aligned and sometimes not at all.

For those who would like to know more about sibling science than I could pack into this book, *The Sibling Effect: What the Bonds Among Brothers and Sisters Reveal About Us* by Jeffrey Kluger (Riverhead Books, 2011) is a good place to start.

All Joy and No Fun: The Paradox of Modern Parenthood by Jennifer Senior (Ecco, 2014) sketches the best portrait of modern parenthood I've read so far. *A Life's Work* by Rachel Cusk (Faber & Faber, 2001) remains one of the most beautiful reflections on early motherhood. *Expecting Better* (Penguin, 2013) and *Cribsheet* (Penguin, 2019) by Emiy Oster do a wonderful job of clarifying and interrogating the science behind some of our deepest-held convictions around pregnancy and parenthood.

The novel *Sight* by Jessie Greengrass (Hogarth, 2018) deals with the countdown to the arrival of a second child, chillingly, beautifully interwoven with reflections on psychoanalysis and the way in which previous generations play into our relationships with our children. Anna Enquist's novel *Contrapunt* (De Arbeiderspers, 2008; translated by Jeannette Ringold as *Counterpoint* [University of Western Australia Press, 2010]) describes life with two growing children—and also the tragic loss of one of them.

Notes

Prologue: Expecting

1 "Een op de honderd moeders heeft meer dan vijf kinderen" [One in one hundred mothers has more than five children], Statistics Netherlands (CBS), May 12, 2017, https://www.cbs.nl/nl-nl /nieuws/2017/19/een-op-de-honderd-moeders-heeft-meer-dan-vijf -kinderen.

2 Tomáš Sobotka and Éva Beaujouan, "Two Is Best? The Persistence of a Two-Child Family Ideal in Europe," *Population and Development Review*, vol. 40, no. 3 (2014), pp. 391–419; Kristen Bialik, "Middle Children Have Become Rarer, but a Growing Share of Americans Now Say Three or More Kids Are 'Ideal,'" *Fact Tank*, August 9, 2018, https://www.pewresearch .org/fact-tank/2018/08/09/middle-children-have-become-rarer -but-a-growing-share-of-americans-now-say-three-or-more -kids-are-ideal/; Lydia Saad, "Americans, in Theory, Think Larger Families Are Ideal," Gallup, July 6, 2018, https:// news.gallup.com/poll/236696/americans-theory-think-larger -families-ideal.aspx.

1. "There's going to be a baby"

1 Helen Keller, *The Story of My Life* (New York, 1903; Project Gutenberg, 2000), chap. 2, https://www.gutenberg.org/files/2397/2397-h /2397-h.htm.

2 Cited in Peter Toohey, *Jealousy* (New Haven, CT: Yale University Press, 2014), p. 16.

3 Kate Spencer, "10 Things No One Tells You About Having a Second Baby," Cosmopolitan.com, May 25, 2016, https://www .cosmopolitan.com/lifestyle/a58880/things-no-one-tells-you -about-second-baby/.

4 Charles Darwin, "A Biographical Sketch of an Infant," *Mind: A Quarterly Review of Psychology and Philosophy*, vol. 2, no. 7 (1877). Reproduced in John van Wyhe (ed.), *The Complete Work of Charles Darwin Online*, http:// darwin-online.org.uk/ (2002).

5 Sybil L. Hart and Maria Legerstee, eds., *Handbook of Jealousy* (West Sussex, UK: Wiley-Blackwell Publishing, 2013), p. x.

6 Toohey, *Jealousy*, p. 23.

7 Sybil Hart and Heather Carrington, "Jealousy in 6-Month-Old Infants," *Infancy*, vol. 3, no. 3 (2002), pp. 395–402.

8 Augustine, *Confessions*, trans. and ed. by Albert C. Outler, 1.7.11, https://www.ling.upenn.edu/courses/hum100/augustinconf.pdf.

9 Peter Stearns, "Jealousy in Western History," *Handbook of Jealousy*, pp. 7–26.

10 Susan Sherwin-White, "Freud on Brothers and Sisters: A Neglected Topic," *Journal of Child Psychotherapy*, vol. 33, no. 1 (2007), p. 8.

11 Robert Sanders, *Sibling Relationships: Theory and Issues for Practice* (New York: Palgrave Macmillan, 2004), p. 55.

12 Sanders, *Sibling Relationships*, p. 56.

13 Peter N. Stearns, "The Rise of Sibling Jealousy in the Twentieth Century," *Symbolic Interaction*, vol. 13, no. 1 (1990), pp. 83–101, esp. p. 91.

14 David W. Lawson and Ruth Mace, "Parental Investment and the Optimization of Human Family Size," *Philosophical Transactions of the Royal Society B*, vol. 366, no. 1563 (2011), pp. 333–43.

15 Nelleke Bakker, "Kibbelen. (Aan een jonge moeder)" [Bickering. (To a young mother)], *De Vrouw* (The woman), March 11, 1899.

16　N. Bakker, J. Noordman, and M. Rietveld-van Wingerden, *Vijf eeuwen opvoeden in Nederland. Idee en praktijk (1500–2000)* [Five centuries of raising children in the Netherlands: Theory and practice (1500–2000)] (Assen: van Gorcum, 2006).

17　Stearns, "The Rise of Sibling Jealousy," p. 90.

2. Bad is stronger than good

1　Laurie Kramer and Katherine J. Conger, "What We Learn from Our Sisters and Brothers: For Better or for Worse," *New Directions for Child and Adolescent Development*, vol. 2009, no. 126 (2009), pp. 1–12, esp. p. 2.

2　Jennifer M. Jenkins and Judy Dunn, "Siblings Within Families: Levels of Analysis and Patterns of Influence," *New Directions for Child and Adolescent Development*, vol. 2009, no. 126 (2009), pp. 79–93.

3　Judy Dunn and Carol Kendrick, "The Arrival of a Sibling: Changes in Patterns of Interaction Between Mother and First-Born Child," *Journal of Child Psychology and Psychiatry*, vol. 21, no. 2 (1980), pp. 119–32.

4　Judy Dunn, Carol Kendrick, and Rosanne MacNamee, "The Reaction of First-Born Children to the Birth of a Sibling: Mothers' Reports," *Journal of Child Psychology and Psychiatry*, vol. 22, no. 1 (1981), pp. 1–18.

5　Frits Boer, *Een gegeven relatie. Over broers en zussen* [A given relationship: On brothers and sisters] (Amsterdam: Prometheus, 1994), p. 27.

6　Brenda L. Volling, "XI. General Discussion: Children's Adjustment and Adaptation Following the Birth of a Sibling," *Monographs of the Society for Research in Child Development*, vol. 82, no. 3 (2017), pp. 142–58.

7　In the Netherlands, the average interval between the birth of first and second children is three years. Among mothers who have a first child later in life, the gap tends to be somewhat smaller; younger mothers on average wait longer to have a second child. "Jonge moeders stellen tweede kind langer uit" [Young mothers postpone second child longer], Statistics Netherlands, December 22, 2011, https:// www.cbs.nl/nl-nl/achtergrond/2011/51/jonge -moeders-stellen-tweede-kindlanger-uit.

8 For instance, in all participating families, both parents lived at home and both mother and child were physically and mentally healthy. The first data collection took place during the pregnancy, so the researchers could not investigate the extent to which the pregnancy itself influenced the eldest. The sample is also American; it's possible that in other countries, where different public amenities are available to young parents, for example, different results would be found.

9 Brenda L. Volling, "I. Introduction: Understanding the Transition to Siblinghood from a Developmental Psychopathology and Ecological Systems Perspective," *Monographs of the Society for Research in Child Development*, vol. 82, no. 3 (2017), pp. 7–25.

10 Roy F. Baumeister et al., "Bad Is Stronger Than Good," *Review of General Psychology*, vol. 5, no. 4 (2001), pp. 323–70.

3. Again, again

1 Jessie Greengrass, *Sight* (New York: Hogarth, 2018), p. 166.

2 For a good summary, read the introduction in Jennifer Senior, *All Joy and No Fun: The Paradox of Modern Parenthood* (New York: Ecco, 2014).

3 Kelly Musick, Ann Meier, and Sarah Flood, "How Parents Fare: Mothers' and Fathers' Subjective Well-Being in Time with Children," *American Sociological Review*, vol. 81, no. 5 (2016), pp. 1069–95.

4 Adam Phillips, *Missing Out: In Praise of the Unlived Life* (New York: Picador, 2013), p. 15.

5 Jean M. Twenge, W. Keith Campbell, and Craig A. Foster, "Parenthood and Marital Satisfaction: A Meta-Analytic Review," *Journal of Marriage and Family*, vol. 65, no. 3 (2003), pp. 574–83.

6 Rachel Margolis and Mikko Myrskylä, "A Global Perspective on Happiness and Fertility," *Population and Development Review*, vol. 37, no. 1 (2011), pp. 29–56. A group of American sociologists who conducted a study among Danish twins even concluded that each child after the first caused mothers a decrease in subjective well-being (for fathers there was no negative effect, but also no positive one). Hans-Peter Kohler, Jere R. Behrman, and Axel Skytthe, "Partner + Children = Happiness? The Effects of Partnerships and Fertility on Well-Being," *Population and Development Review*, vol. 31, no. 3 (September 2005), pp. 407–45.

7 The finding that having more children brings, on average, more unhappiness mainly applied to parents under forty. When the parents were over forty, an extra child also made them extra happy. Margolis and Myrskylä, "A Global Perspective," p. 29.

8 "De samenhang tussen geluk en het krijgen van kinderen" [The connection between happiness and having children], Statistics Netherlands, March 11, 2013, https://www.cbs.nl/nl -nl/achtergrond/ 2013/11/de-samenhang-tussen-geluk-en-het -krijgen-van-kinderen.

9 Statistics Netherlands made use of survey results from the Permanent Quality of Life Survey (Permanent onderzoek naar de leefsituatie, POLS) between 1998 and 2009, encompassing approximately 112,000 respondents. They were asked to indicate how happy they were and how satisfied they felt with their lives. The study therefore compared parents in different periods of parenthood; individual parents were not followed over time. The study among British and German citizens made use of data from the British Household Panel Survey (2,689 respondents between 1991 and 2008) and the German Socio-Economic Panel (around 4,500 respondents between 1984 and 2009), respectively. These studies had fewer participants, but they *were* followed up longitudinally, so it is possible to map out the subjective well-being of the same individual before and after having first, second, and third children.

10 Mikko Myrskylä and Rachel Margolis, "Happiness: Before and After the Kids," *Demography*, vol. 51, no. 5 (2014), pp. 1843–66.

11 Zadie Smith, "Joy," *New York Review of Books*, January 10, 2013, https://www.nybooks.com/articles/2013/01/10/joy/.

12 The press release can be found at: http://www.lse.ac.uk/website -archive/newsAndMedia/newsArchives/2014/10/ChildrenAnd Happiness.aspx.

13 Marc Wittmann, *Felt Time: The Science of How We Experience Time*, trans. Erik Butler (Cambridge, MA: MIT Press, 2017), p. 87.

14 Rachel Cusk, *A Life's Work: On Becoming a Mother* (London: Faber & Faber, 2001), p. 136.

15 Greengrass, *Sight*, p. 155.

16 Anna-Karin Klint Carlander et al., "Impact of Clinical Factors and Personality on the Decision to Have a Second Child. Longitudinal Cohort-Study of First-Time Mothers," *Acta Obstetricia*

et Gynecologica Scandinavica, vol. 93, no. 2 (2014), pp. 182–88, esp. p. 186.

17 Douwe Draaisma, *Forgetting: Myths, Perils and Compensations*, trans. Liz Waters (New Haven, CT: Yale University Press, 2015), p. 11.

4. A fly buzzing around my ear

1 "The main reason parents mention for choosing to have a second child," writes the child psychiatrist Frits Boer, "is that they don't want their eldest child to end up alone." Boer, *Een gegeven relatie* [A given relationship], p. 20.

2 Karl König, *Brothers and Sisters: The Order of Birth in the Family* (Edinburgh: Floris Books, 2014), p. 25. (Previously published as *Brothers and Sisters: A Study in Child Psychology* [Onex, Switzerland: The Camphill Movement, 1977].)

3 "It's thought that only children are less happy than children with brothers and sisters, that an only child risks developing a selfish, egotistical character and having trouble making friends." Boer, *Een gegeven relatie* [A given relationship], p. 20.

4 Toni Falbo and Denise F. Polit, "Quantitative Review of the Only Child Literature: Research Evidence and Theory Development," *Psychological Bulletin*, vol. 100, no. 2 (1986), pp. 176–89. See also: Lauren Sandler, *One and Only: The Freedom of Having an Only Child, and the Joy of Being One* (New York: Simon & Schuster, 2013).

5 Boer, *Een gegeven relatie* [A given relationship], p. 106.

6 In some respects, only children are actually at an advantage. For instance, research shows that only children are read to more often in childhood, more often attend music or dance classes, and more often go on trips abroad than children with brothers or sisters. Boer, *Een gegeven relatie* [A given relationship], p. 106.

7 Kohler, Behrman, and Skytthe, "Partner + Children = Happiness?"

8 Judy Dunn, "Sibling Relationships in Early Childhood," *Child Development*, vol. 54, no. 4 (1983), pp. 787–811, p. 793.

9 Scott Forbes, *A Natural History of Families* (Princeton, NJ: Princeton University Press, 2005), p. 197.

10 Susan M. McHale, Kimberly A. Updegraff, and Shawn D. Whiteman, "Sibling Relationships and Influences in Childhood

and Adolescence," *Journal of Marriage and Family*, vol. 74, no. 5 (2012), pp. 913–30.

11 McHale, Updegraff, and Whiteman, "Sibling Relationships and Influences," pp. 919–21.

12 Laurie Kramer, phone conversation with author, March 28, 2018.

13 Kirsten L. Buist, Maja Deković, and Peter Prinzie, "Sibling Relationship Quality and Psychopathology of Children and Adolescents: A Meta-Analysis," *Clinical Psychology Review*, vol. 33, no .1 (2013), pp. 97–106.

14 Geoffrey L. Greif and Michael E. Woolley, *Adult Sibling Relationships* (New York: Columbia University Press, 2016), p. 71.

15 Sheila van Berkel, "Growing Up Together" (PhD diss., Leiden University, 2015), p. 74.

16 There are many studies that look into the influence of siblings on substance abuse or deviant behavior. Often, that influence turns out to be mediated by the sibling relationship quality as well as parental behavior. For the effect of an elder sister's teen pregnancy on younger sisters, see, for instance, Patricia L. East et al., "How an Adolescent's Childbearing Affects Siblings' Pregnancy Risk: A Qualitative Study of Mexican American Youths," *Perspectives on Sexual and Reproductive Health*, vol. 41, no. 4 (2009), pp. 210–17.

See also: Abigail A. Fagan and Jake M. Najman, "The Relative Contributions of Parental and Sibling Substance Use to Adolescent Tobacco, Alcohol, and Other Drug Use," *Journal of Drug Issues*, vol. 35, no. 4 (2005), pp. 869–84; and Sabina Low, Joann Wu Shortt, and James Snyder, "Sibling Influences on Adolescent Substance Use: The Role of Modeling, Collusion, and Conflict," *Development and Psychopathology*, vol. 24, no.1 (2012), pp. 287–300.

17 Thomas Ewin Smith, "Academic Achievement and Teaching Younger Siblings," *Social Psychology Quarterly*, vol. 53, no. 4 (1990), pp. 352–63; and Nina Howe et al., "'The driver doesn't sit, he stands up like the Flintstones!': Sibling Teaching During Teacher-Directed and Self-Guided Tasks," *Journal of Cognition and Development*, vol. 13, no. 2 (2012), pp. 208–31.

18 Alison M. O'Connor and Angela D. Evans, "The Relation Between Having Siblings and Children's Cheating and Lie-Telling

Behaviors," *Journal of Experimental Child Psychology*, vol. 168 (2018), pp. 49–60.

19   Alexander C. Jensen and Susan M. McHale, "Mothers', Fathers', and Siblings' Perceptions of Parents' Differential Treatment of Siblings: Links with Family Relationship Qualities," *Journal of Adolescence*, vol. 60 (2017), pp. 119–29.

20   The effect goes further than that of shared genes or divorced parents, for instance. Elise de Vuijst et al., "Cross-Sibling Effects on Divorce in the Netherlands," *Advances in Life Course Research*, vol. 34 (2017), pp. 1–9.

21   Rosalind Edwards, Lucy Hadfield, Helen Lucey, and Melanie Mauthner, *Sibling Identity and Relationships: Sisters and Brothers* (New York: Routledge, 2006), pp. 81–82.

5. A pack, a tribe, a tornado

1   Michael Harris, *Solitude: In Pursuit of a Singular Life in a Crowded World* (New York: Thomas Dunne Books, 2017).

2   Anna Enquist, *Contrapunt* (De Arbeiderspers, 2008; translated by Jeannette Ringold as *Counterpoint* [University of Western Australia Press, 2010]), p. 70.

6. Thou shalt not compare

1   Cusk, *A Life's Work*, p. 136.

2   Laurie Kramer and Lisa A. Baron, "Intergenerational Linkages: How Experiences with Siblings Relate to the Parenting of Siblings," *Journal of Social and Personal Relationships*, vol. 12, no. 1 (1995), pp. 67–87.

3   This is also the point made by Judith Rich Harris in *The Nurture Assumption: Why Children Turn Out the Way They Do* (New York: Free Press, 2009). Children, she claims, do not become who they become through their parents' actions alone. In her view, it is *other children*—friends, classmates—who determine a person's social development. Moreover: "The way a parent acts toward a particular child depends on the child's age, physical appearance, current behavior, past behavior, intelligence, and state of health," Harris writes. "Parents tailor their child-rearing style to the individual child. Child-rearing is not something a parent does to a child: it is something the parent and the child do together" (p. 23).

7. Typical second child

1 Petter Kristensen and Tor Bjerkedal, "Explaining the Relation Between Birth Order and Intelligence," *Science*, vol. 316, no. 5832 (2007), p. 1717.

2 In Galton's story, daughters scarcely had a role to play—which also fitted the mores of his time. Galton later built up the less-than-illustrious reputation of being the founder of eugenics, the belief that the human race can be improved by selective "breeding."

3 David W. Lawson, "The Behavioural Ecology of Modern Families: A Longitudinal Study of Parental Investment and Child Development" (PhD thesis, University College London, 2009), p. 30.

4 The desire to avoid splitting family property weighed more heavily than the need to allow each son to build up an autonomous existence. Naomi J. Miller and Naomi Yavneh, eds., *Sibling Relations and Gender in the Early Modern World: Sisters, Brothers and Others* (London: Ashgate, 2006), p. 3.

5 If there are two or three sons in a fairy tale, then you can be sure all hell's going to break loose—and in particular that the youngest will be treated horribly by his elder brothers. The sociologist Lily E. Clerkx ascribes this to the early modern inheritance system: the first was the heir, the second could often marry a daughter with a dowry, but as the third son you got nothing. Lily E. Clerkx, *En ze leefden nog lang en gelukkig. Familieleven in sprookjes. Een historisch-sociologische benadering* [And they lived happily ever after. Family life in fairy tales. A historical-sociological approach] (Amsterdam: Bert Bakker, 1992).

6 The quote, from the historian Jack Goody, is taken from Clerkx, *En ze leefden nog lang en gelukkig*, p. 174.

7 Julia M. Rohrer, Boris Egloff, and Stefan C. Schmukle, "Examining the Effects of Birth Order on Personality," *Proceedings of the National Academy of Sciences*, vol. 112, no. 46 (2015), pp. 14224–29.

8 Roger D. Clark and Glenn A. Rice, "Family Constellations and Eminence: The Birth Orders of Nobel Prize Winners," *Journal of Psychology*, vol. 110, no. 2 (1982), pp. 281–87.

9 Daniel S. P. Schubert, Mazie E. Wagner, and Herman J. P. Schubert, "Family Constellation and Creativity: Firstborn Predominance Among Classical Music Composers," *Journal of Psychology*, vol. 95, no. 1 (1977), pp. 147–49.

10   W. Scott Terry, "Birth Order and Prominence in the History of Psychology," *Psychological Record*, vol. 39, no. 3 (1989), pp. 333–37.

11   Frank J. Sulloway, *Born to Rebel: Birth Order, Family Dynamics, and Creative Lives* (New York: Vintage Books, 1997), pp. 262, 324–25.

12   König, *Brothers and Sisters*, p. 26.

13   Nicholas C. Herrera et al., "Beliefs About Birth Rank and Their Reflection in Reality," *Journal of Personality and Social Psychology*, vol. 85, no. 1 (2003), pp. 142–50.

14   Rodica Ioana Damian and Brent W. Roberts, "The Associations of Birth Order with Personality and Intelligence in a Representative Sample of U.S. High School Students," *Journal of Research in Personality*, vol. 58 (2015), pp. 96–105.

15   Rohrer, Egloff, and Schmukle, "Examining the Effects of Birth Order on Personality," pp. 14224–29.

16   Rodica Ioana Damian and Brent W. Roberts, "Settling the Debate on Birth Order and Personality," *Proceedings of the National Academy of Sciences*, vol. 112, no. 46 (2015), pp. 14119–20.

17   Albert Somit, Steven A. Peterson, and Alan Arwine, "Birth Order and Political Behavior: Clearing the Underbrush," *International Political Science Review*, vol. 14, no. 2 (1993), pp. 149–60, esp. p. 149.

8. Shall we read a story together?

1   H. M. Wolsk et al., "Siblings Promote a Type 1/Type 17–oriented Immune Response in the Airways of Asymptomatic Neonates," *Allergy*, vol. 71, no. 6 (2016), pp. 820–28.

2   Ahila Ayyavoo et al., "First-Born Children Have Reduced Insulin Sensitivity and Higher Daytime Blood Pressure Compared to Later-Born Children," *Journal of Clinical Endocrinology and Metabolism*, vol. 98, no. 3 (2013), pp. 1248–53.

3   A long-running study among British people showed that only children at ten were on average 27.5 mm taller than children with one sibling, 29.2 mm taller than children with two siblings, 30.8 mm taller than children with three, and 31.5 mm taller than those with four. David W. Lawson and Ruth Mace, "Sibling Configuration and Childhood Growth in Contemporary British Families," *International Journal of Epidemiology*, vol. 37, no. 6 (2008), pp. 1408–21. See also: Tim Savage et al., "Birth Order Progressively

Affects Childhood Height," *Clinical Endocrinology*, vol. 79, no. 3 (2013), pp. 379–85; and: Mikko Myrskylä et al., "The Association Between Height and Birth Order: Evidence from 652,518 Swedish Men," *Journal of Epidemiology and Community Health*, vol. 67, no. 7 (2013), pp. 571–77.

4 Lawson and Mace, "Sibling Configuration and Childhood Growth," p. 1419.

5 David W. Lawson and Ruth Mace, "Siblings and Childhood Mental Health: Evidence for a Later-Born Advantage," *Social Science & Medicine*, vol. 70, no. 12 (2010), pp. 2061–69.

6 Lawson, "The Behavioural Ecology of Modern Families," p. 173.

7 For an overview, see: Kieron J. Barclay, "The Birth Order Paradox: Sibling Differences in Educational Attainment," *Research in Social Stratification and Mobility*, vol. 54 (2018), pp. 56–65.

8 Norway has compulsory military service for men, and recruits are standardly subjected to a series of medical and psychological tests, including IQ tests. Economists analyzed the results of all Norwegian men born between 1967 and 1998. Sandra E. Black, Paul J. Devereux, and Kjell G. Salvanes, "Older and Wiser? Birth Order and the IQ of Young Men," IZA Discussion Paper No. 3007 (2007).

9 And things went downhill from there: "Compared to the first-born, third- and fourth-borns are 10 and 18 percentage points less likely to graduate high school and complete about 1 to 1.5 fewer years of education." Jee-Yeon K. Lehmann, Ana Nuevo-Chiquero, and Marian Vidal-Fernandez, "The Early Origins of Birth Order Differences in Children's Outcomes and Parental Behavior," *Journal of Human Resources*, vol. 53, no. 1 (2018), pp. 123–56.

10 Joseph Price, "Parent-Child Quality Time: Does Birth Order Matter?," *Journal of Human Resources*, vol. 43, no. 1 (2008), pp. 240–65.

11 Ana Nuevo-Chiquero and Marian Vidal-Fernandez, "How Parents Shape the Advantages of Being First-Born," *The Conversation*, November 2, 2016, https:// theconversation.com/how-parents -shape-the-advantages-of-being-firstborn-67644.

12 Monique de Haan, Erik Plug, and José Rosero, "Birth Order and Human Capital Development: Evidence from Ecuador," IZA Discussion Paper No. 6706 (2012).

13 Kristensen and Bjerkedal, "Birth Order and Intelligence," p. 1717.

14 Barclay, "The Birth Order Paradox," p. 57.

15   Barclay, "The Birth Order Paradox," p. 57.

16   Sandra E. Black, "New Evidence on the Impacts of Birth Order," *NBER Reporter 2017*, no. 4, https://www.nber.org/reporter/2017number4/black.html.

17   When it comes to temperament, behavioral problems, and other noncognitive factors, the researchers found no difference between first and subsequent children, with one single exception: first children in general had more self-confidence and more highly estimated their abilities than second and subsequent children—especially when it came to their own school abilities. Lehmann, Nuevo-Chiquero, and Vidal-Fernandez, "The Early Origins of Birth Order Differences," p. 138.

18   Lehmann, Nuevo-Chiquero, and Vidal-Fernandez, "The Early Origins of Birth Order Differences," p. 150.

19   Lehmann, Nuevo-Chiquero, and Vidal-Fernandez, "The Early Origins of Birth Order Differences," p. 151.

20   Lehmann, Nuevo-Chiquero, and Vidal-Fernandez, "The Early Origins of Birth Order Differences," p. 151.

9. Time is a currency

1   Berenice Monna and Anne H. Gauthier, "A Review of the Literature on the Social and Economic Determinants of Parental Time," *Journal of Family and Economic Issues*, vol. 29, no. 4 (2008), pp. 634–53, esp. p. 638.

2   Enquist, *Contrapunt* [*Counterpoint*], p. 14.

3   The explanation generally given is that caring for children in Western societies is seen as the task of the mother. Since the 1970s, fathers have played an ever greater role, and the difference between maternal time and paternal time has shrunk. Monna and Gauthier, "A Review of the Literature," p. 639.

4   Anne Roeters, ed., *Alle ballen in de lucht. Tijdsbesteding in Nederland en de samenhang met kwaliteit van leven* [All the balls in the air: Time allocation in the Netherlands and the association with quality of life], Netherlands Institute for Social Research (SCP), December 7, 2018, p. 105.

5   Joke Smit, "Het onbehagen bij de vrouw" [Women's discontent], *De Gids*, November 1967, pp. 267–81. I consulted an online version here: http://www.emancipatie.nl/_documenten/js/werk/het onbehagenbijdevrouw/hetonbehagenbijdevrouw.pdf.

6 Suzanne M. Bianchi, "Maternal Employment and Time with Children: Dramatic Change or Surprising Continuity?," *Demography*, vol. 37, no. 4 (2000), pp. 401–14.

7 Bianchi, "Maternal Employment and Time with Children," p. 401.

8 Bianchi speculates that the availability of contraception has made parenthood a conscious choice for a higher proportion of parents and that these parents also like to spend plenty of time with their children. It's also less overwhelming to do so, because on average people have fewer children: "It takes fewer years to rear one or two children to school age than to do the same for three or four children," Bianchi points out. Increased urbanization is another possible explanation: parents lose more time keeping an eye on their children and transporting them to friends and extracurricular activities, because cities in general and traffic in particular are seen as a greater danger. Liana C. Sayer, Suzanne M. Bianchi, and John P. Robinson, "Are Parents Investing Less in Children? Trends in Mothers' and Fathers' Time with Children," *American Journal of Sociology*, vol. 110, no. 1 (2004), pp. 1–43.

9 An international comparison shows that parents in other industrialized countries since the 1960s have spent more time on their children. Anne H. Gauthier, Timothy M. Smeeding, and Frank F. Furstenberg Jr., "Are Parents Investing Less Time in Children? Trends in Selected Industrialized Countries," *Population and Development Review*, vol. 30, no. 4 (2004), pp. 647–71.

10 Giulia M. Dotti Sani and Judith Treas, "Educational Gradients in Parents' Child-Care Time Across Countries, 1965–2012," *Journal of Marriage and Family*, vol. 78, no. 4 (2016), pp. 1083–96.

11 Roeters, *Alle ballen in de lucht* [All the balls in the air], pp. 107–9 and 115.

12 And the more children a couple has, the more the parents lose sleep: "Unlike most other types of time allocation, there is a direct relationship between the number of children in a family and the reduction of adult sleep time." Lyn Craig, *Contemporary Motherhood: The Impact of Children on Adult Time* (London: Ashgate, 2007), p. 37.

13 Cusk, *A Life's Work*, p. 141.

14 Bianchi, "Maternal Employment and Time with Children," p. 401.

15 Kim Parker and Wendy Wang, "Modern Parenthood: Roles of Moms and Dads Converge as They Balance Work and Family" (Washington, DC: Pew Research Center, 2013), p. 6.

16 The question was put to parents whose child was under nine years of age. Roeters, *Alle ballen in de lucht* [All the balls in the air], p. 106.

17 Roeters, *Alle ballen in de lucht* [All the balls in the air], p. 109.

18 Laura Norkin, "How Much of Having a Second Kid Is a Career Choice?," *The Cut*, May 11, 2018, https://www.thecut.com/2018/05/how-money-could-stop-me-from-having-a-second-kid.html.

19 Henrik Kleven, Camille Landais, and Jakob Egholt Søgaard, "Children and Gender Inequality: Evidence from Denmark," NBER Working Paper No. 24219 (2018), p. 50.

20 An American study published in 2004 calculated that a second baby costs the mother only six minutes' extra care time per day (Monna and Gauthier, "A Review of the Literature," p. 641). An Australian study from 2007 found that a second child costs a family an extra hour per day. It's not only the primary and inter-active care that increase in quantity, according to the author, but also "child-related travel and communication time." See: Craig, *Contemporary Motherhood*, pp. 30–31.

21 Chiara Monfardini and Sarah Grace See, "Birth Order and Child Cognitive Outcomes: An Exploration of the Parental Time Mechanism," *Education Economics*, vol. 24, no. 5 (2016), pp. 481–95, esp. p. 482.

22 David Lawson, "The Behavioural Ecology of Modern Families," p. 81.

23 In this study, "quality time" was defined as the time "in which the child was the primary focus of the activity or in which there would be a reasonable amount of interaction." Examples of quality time activities include reading together, playing, helping with homework, doing crafts, eating, and participating in religious activities. Monfardini and See, "Birth Order and Child Cognitive Outcomes," pp. 486, 491.

24 Nazli Baydar, April Greek, and R. Mark Gritz, "Young Mothers' Time Spent at Work and Time Spent Caring for Children," *Journal of Family and Economic Issues*, vol. 20 (1999), pp. 61–84. Cited in Monna and Gauthier, "A Review of the Literature," p. 641.

10. Long days, short years

1 Ralph LaRossa, "The Transition to Parenthood and the Social Reality of Time," *Journal of Marriage and Family*, vol. 45, no. 3 (1983), pp. 579–89, esp. p. 579.

2   Smit, "Het onbehagen bij de vrouw" [Women's discontent], p. 270.

3   Jenny Offill, *Dept. of Speculation* (London: Granta, 2015), pp. 25–26.

4   Enquist, *Contrapunt* [*Counterpoint*], p. 14.

5   Valeria Luiselli, *Faces in the Crowd*, trans. Christina MacSweeney (London: Granta, 2013), p. 4.

6   All over the world, "temporal units" of around three seconds form the building blocks of music and poetry—think of the Beatles' "Hey Jude," or "da da da daaaa" in Ludwig van Beethoven's Fifth Symphony. Longer than that, and you no longer parse them as a single unit. Wittmann, *Felt Time*, pp. 44–50.

7   The Netherlands Institute for Social Research (SCP) shows that the older children become, the less time their parents spend caring for them and supervising them. A child aged 0 to 3 costs 9.4 hours per week of care and supervision from fathers and 16.4 from mothers. For a child aged 4 to 11 that's 4.3 and 7.4 hours, respectively, and aged 12 to 17 just 0.8 and 1.4 hours. It's particularly the care for small children that's routine, predictable, and fairly inflexible. Roeters, *Alle ballen in de lucht* [All the balls in the air], p. 112.

8   Zadie Smith, "Elegy for a Country's Seasons," *New York Review of Books*, April 3, 2014, https://www.nybooks.com/articles/2014/04/03/elegy-countrys-seasons/.

9   Matthias Doepke, "Gary Becker on the Quantity and Quality of Children," *Journal of Demographic Economics*, vol. 81, no. 1 (2015), pp. 59–66.

10 Nancy Folbre, *Valuing Children: Rethinking the Economics of the Family* (Cambridge, MA: Harvard University Press, 2008), p. 28.

11. The siren song of the easy baby

1   Hippolyte d'Albis, Paula E. Gobbi, and Angela Greulich, "Having a Second Child and Access to Childcare: Evidence from European Countries," *Journal of Demographic Economics*, vol. 83, no. 2 (2017), pp. 177–210.

2   Ari Klaengur Jónsson, "The Effects of the Parental Leave Reform and the Economic Crisis on Childbearing Behavior in Iceland at the Dawn of a New Millennium," *Families and Societies Working Paper Series 60* (2016), p. 6.

3   Markus Jokela, "Characteristics of the First Child Predict the Parents' Probability of Having Another Child," *Developmental Psychology*, vol. 46, no. 4 (2010), pp. 915–26.

4 Winston Chang (@winston_chang), "If there's a baby boom in 9 months, it'll consist entirely of first-born children," Twitter, March 24, 2020, 1:45 p.m., https://twitter.com/winston_chang /status/1242507862229676033.

5 Sarah Conly, *One Child: Do We Have a Right to More?* (New York: Oxford University Press, 2016), p. 5.

6 GBD 2017 Population and Fertility Collaborators, "Population and Fertility by Age and Sex for 195 Countries and Territories, 1950–2017: A Systematic Analysis for the Global Burden of Disease Study 2017," *The Lancet*, vol. 392, no. 10159 (2018), pp. 1995–2051, esp. p. 1995.

7 Paul Hawken, ed., *Drawdown: The Most Comprehensive Plan Ever Proposed to Reverse Global Warming* (New York: Penguin Books, 2017), pp. 78–81.

8 Seth Wynes and Kimberly A. Nicholas, "The Climate Mitigation Gap: Education and Government Recommendations Miss the Most Effective Individual Actions," *Environmental Research Letters*, vol. 12, no. 7 (2017), p. 3.

Epilogue: On expectations

1 Lydia Davis, *Varieties of Disturbance* (New York: Farrar, Straus & Giroux, 2007), pp. 115–24.

2 Alexander C. Jensen and Susan M. McHale, "What Makes Siblings Different? The Development of Sibling Differences in Academic Achievement and Interests," *Journal of Family Psychology*, vol. 29, no. 3 (2015), pp. 469–78.

3 Only if the eldest was a boy and the youngest a girl did the parents say that the youngest was more capable. This also applied to school grades. Jensen and McHale, "What Makes Siblings Different?," pp. 472, 475.

4 V. Joseph Hotz and Juan Pantano, "Strategic Parenting, Birth Order and School Performance," *Journal of Population Economics*, vol. 28, no. 4 (2015), pp. 911–36.

5 Alex Jensen and Susan M. McHale, "What Makes Siblings from the Same Family So Different? Parents," *The Conversation*, July 6, 2015, https://theconversation. com/what-makes-siblings-from -the-same-family-so-different-parents-44071.

6 Katharina A. Schwarz, Roland Pfister, and Christian Büchel, "Rethinking Explicit Expectations: Connecting Placebos, Social

Cognition, and Contextual Perception," *Trends in Cognitive Sciences*, vol. 20, no. 6 (2016), pp. 469–80.

7 Schwarz, Pfister, and Büchel, "Rethinking Explicit Expectation," p. 470.

8 There are studies that show that parents had certain expectations of their children even before the birth, and that the nature of those expectations predicted how they saw their children once they were born. Scientists, for instance, asked almost one hundred expectant parents to recall memories of their own childhood; fathers who described their own childhood positively and in terms of growth also later had a more positive image of their children than fathers who had more negative or anxious recollections of childhood. Erika M. Manczak et al., "Autobiographical Memories of Childhood and Sources of Subjectivity in Parents' Perceptions of Infant Temperament," *Infant Behavior and Development*, vol. 44 (2016), pp. 77–85.

Acknowledgments

Thank you Milou Klein Lankhorst, Harminke Medendorp, and Andreas Jonkers for making the first (Dutch) iteration of this book possible. Thank you Judith van IJken, Jesse Frederik, Marjolijn van Heemstra, Jelmer Mommers, Anoek Nuyens, Nina Polak, Jona Specker, and Sophie van Winden for helping me improve on early drafts.

Thank you Petronella Bakker, Gijs Beets, Sheila van Berkel, Kirsten Buist, Heleen de Hertog, Alex Jensen, Janneke Kemner, Gerard Koppelman, Laurie Kramer, Anne Roeters, and Marc Wittmann for sharing your time and expertise. Sheila, Kirsten, and Anne: double thanks for reading and commenting on a draft version of this book.

Thank you Rebecca Carter and Emma Parry of Janklow & Nesbit for taking this book overseas.

Thank you Hannah MacDonald for first allowing this book to have a second life in English; thank you Travis Mushett for coming up with the English title; and thank you Anna Asbury for translating it with amazing sensitivity, patience, and grace.

Thank you Caroline Zancan, Kerry Cullen, Hannah Campbell, and everyone else at Henry Holt for giving this book such a warm welcome in the United States.

Thank you Sanne Berger for lending your voice and sharing your memories, for reading and commenting on an early draft, and for three decades of sisterhood.

To all fathers and mothers I know: thank you for sharing your experiences and cogitations. And to my own: thank you for your love, your interest, your care. Endlessly many thanks, also, for having a second child.

My greatest gratitude, too great for words, but of which I hope this book forms a modest expression, is to Maarten, Eliza, and Oscar. Thank you for everything, and forever.

About the Author

Lynn Berger is a staff writer at online journalism platform *De Correspondent*, where she covers language and culture. She holds a PhD in communications from Columbia University and lives in Amsterdam, the Netherlands. *Second Thoughts* is her first book.